JUST ONE MORE DANCE

JUST ONE MORE DANCE

A Story of Degradation and Fear, Faith and Compassion
from a Survivor of the Nazi Death Camps

ERNEST LEVY

MAINSTREAM
PUBLISHING

EDINBURGH AND LONDON

First published in Great Britain in 1998 by
MAINSTREAM PUBLISHING COMPANY (EDINBURGH) LTD
7 Albany Street
Edinburgh EH1 3UG

ISBN 1 84018 134 6

A catalogue record for this book is available from the British Library

Typeset in Van Dijck MT
Printed and bound in Great Britain by Butler and Tanner Ltd

To my grandchildren Ari and Malki

VESSEL OF LIGHT

Your told us of your life. How
from Hungary to Slovakia
your father sought a future:
from Bratislava to a border
the red buses took your people.
Your march was towards a distant light.
In Budapest, head down, until
they came with wagons, railed you to
Auschwitz – the air, the hellish
faces, little breath but fear and
the sounds of torment – of Selection.
To Birkenau – to claim a tin,
that was a light, a holy song.
To show it yet and sing out still.
A paper trumpet blamed Jews, brought
Helmut and a drink to share with Joe.
The march north to Bergen-Belsen
met a farmer Max who asked, 'Let
me give these poor people one potato a day.'
That skin, that flesh, that heat
meant you could use your elbow to
raise your head from Belsen's dead ground
and cry out your existence to the soldiers,
to the nurse who spoon-fed you back
to where your family had been.

Mary Barrett, 17 February 1997

CONTENTS

~

THANKS TO SPONSORS

~

The Reverend Ernest Levy and Mainstream Publishing would like to thank the Scottish Jewish Archives Committee and the European Jewish Publications Society for their generous assistance with this project.

The Scottish Jewish Archives Committee is responsible for the collection of the history of all aspects of the Jews in Scotland. The EJPS is a registered charity which makes grants to assist in the publication and distribution of books relevant to Jewish literature, history, religion, philosophy, politics and culture. They can be contacted at EJPS, 1st Floor, 37-43 Sackville Street, London W1X 2DL.

ACKNOWLEDGEMENTS

~

Writing this book has taken much time and energy and I am grateful to many good friends who have assisted me in bringing this work to its conclusion. Dr Kenneth Collins conceived the idea of publishing these recollections and his partnership with Dr Ben Braber, under the auspices of the Scottish Jewish Archives Committee, has ensured that the project was carried out professionally and effectively.

John Linklater has believed in this book from the outset and has made his advice freely available throughout. This has ensured that the text reflects my material faithfully while smoothing out its flow. Mia Stevenson has helped me recall these terrible events and collect my memories into narrative form.

I am also grateful to the Executive, Council and members of the Giffnock and Newlands Synagogue for their support for this project symbolising the harmonious relationship existing within the Synagogue for over thirty years. The Glasgow Jewish Representative Council has also assisted with the project and some of the material was originally presented at Holocaust Memorial Meetings held under their auspices.

Finally, I should like to record my appreciation of those who helped the project in its crucial early stages and ensured that it would proceed to its conclusion. Therefore, I would like to say thank you to Geoffrey Ognall, Mark Goldberg, the Livingstone family, Leslie Wolfson and Dr. Dickie Wolfson and Victor and Harvey Fields.

FOREWORD
by Sir Harry Secombe

~

In 1984 when I was presenting a religious series *Highway* I had to travel up to Scotland to broadcast a programme from Glasgow. In each show I would interview various people in the place I was visiting, and one interviewee was cantor Ernest Levy. The story he had to tell was intensely moving, reducing all of us, even the hard-boiled camera crew, to tears. He spoke simply about his experiences at the hands of the Nazis: how he had been in seven different concentration camps, escaping from Belsen from under a pile of bodies.

What was remarkable about his story was his lack of bitterness about what had happened to him and his forgiveness for those who had been his persecutors. His shining sincerity made a lasting impression on me and we have kept in touch ever since that day.

Ernest is an object lesson to us all – a man of infinite compassion in these days of gathering hatreds and prejudices.

He is a great inspiration for anyone who has suffered under oppression – an indomitable spirit who has experienced unimaginable hardship and come through with his faith in the essential goodness of mankind still unshaken.

A man of SHALOM [peace].

Sir Harry Secombe, 1998

AUTHOR'S NOTE

~

Many of the events I have described in this book took place over fifty years ago. It may be that there are some minor errors in my recollection of specific details of what occurred, but I am sure that if any errors have been recorded they are few indeed.

I

JUST ONE MORE DANCE

~

The knock on the door came on 4 November 1938.

Friday night, the family was seated at the table, ready for our traditional Sabbath meal. We did not expect trouble. There had been rumours, but there had been rumours before. By 1938 the Jews in Europe had been used to living in fear. We waited for the storm clouds to gather, thinking they would disappear as they always had before. A second rap on the door meant we had waited too long. They had finally come for us.

I was 13 at the time, the youngest of the eight children of Leopold Löwy and Therezia Hauser - an ordinary Jewish family in Bratislava, the capital of Slovakia which, at the time, formed part of the Czechoslovak Republic.

Although my elder brother Karl, later called Charles, was spending some time in Germany, our family was still together. Next to father at the white-clothed table sat Max, the eldest, the bohemian of the family, born in 1910, and one year older than the musical Karl and also older brother of the impulsive Fritz (born 1914). Then the girls, Hedwig, a born lady (1917), vivacious Else (1920) and sensuous Lillie (1921). After them came Alexander (1923), an academically brilliant boy. I was the last, number eight, the child who should not have been.

Following Alexander's difficult birth in 1923, the doctor had warned my mother against having any more children. She was already forty-two and having another child would seriously jeopardise her health. So, when mother discovered that my arrival was imminent, she called a family council.

The Löwy household operated as a team and the older siblings always had a part to play in these conferences. Mother told me later what had been discussed. According to her, the family decided that the best course of action would be to consult Rabbi Akiva Shreiber – a famous holy man who came from a long line of great sages.

'Don't worry,' Rabbi Shreiber had assured my father. 'Heavenly protection is at hand. There is absolutely nothing to worry about. What's more – you will have a boy.'

For my father, the rabbi's word was all he needed. If he had been a more pragmatic individual, I would never have come into this world. As it was, on Friday, 13 January 1925, I exchanged the cosy comfort and security of my mother's womb for the realities of the outside world which I soon discovered to be contradictory, sometimes stimulating and, at other times, hostile and merciless.

My birth coincided with the family moving to a beautiful home, complete with a garden full of flowers. This garden was a real novelty for our family. My brothers and sisters had all grown up in a dark house in the Jewish ghetto in the centre of Bratislava. As my father achieved some business success working as an agent for a woollen manufacturer, his employers helped him to acquire a better house in the Czech quarter of town.

Our luxurious new home – with a novelty: an inside lavatory – was situated in the Schanzstrasse. We lived on the ground floor of the two-storey building, while the other three flats in the house were rented out to different families. Father also needed the house for his business. He used part of the basement and the massive loft as offices and to store his papers and swatches of material.

The move to the Schanzstrasse was the crown on father's career. Leopold Löwy had been born in the tiny Hungarian village of Kapuvar from where the family moved to the town of Papa in north-west Hungary near the Danube. Papa was a small, predominantly Jewish settlement, where my grandfather, Eliezer, served as cantor – the synagogue official who leads the congregation in prayer. My father was the eldest of five brothers and sisters.

Father's achievements in selling cloth made him the 'golden calf' of the family. Indeed, the move to the Czech quarter of Bratislava meant a vast improvement in our standard of living.

A stone's throw from the Schanzstrasse was the countryside, a welcome change from the ghetto, and the Czech quarter was affluent. Its inhabitants were house-proud and the neighbourhood was carefully controlled by the local authorities. If you did not sweep and wash the pavement outside your house, you could be fined up to 50 krona. We did not regard sweeping as too much of a chore, as we enjoyed going out with the watering can, sprinkling the pavement and brushing it clean.

My brother Alexander, who we used to call Munky, and I were inseparable, despite the difference in our temperaments. We shared a bedroom in the new house, with a large and comfortable mahogany bed under the window in which we could sleep head to toe. Munky was a moralist. When I fell in love with a different girl every day of the week, he made it clear that this was a practice that he would never approve of. In addition, I was regarded as the clown of the family, playing pranks and mimicking people, while Munky was the serious one with a natural talent for learning, especially foreign languages. But he was also a great football player and both of us enjoyed participating in various matches organised between the different neighbourhoods in Bratislava.

Munky, Lillie, Else and I – being the four youngest children – formed a unit within the family. We did everything together and our favourite pastime was going out for excursions into the countryside with other children from the neighbourhood, such as Helmut Palme, a young German boy from the Schanzstrasse, who was constantly in our house. A real treat was when Kalman Hilvert, one of the older boys, came along on our excursions. Then mother would allow us to stay overnight in a youth hostel.

Inside the flat mother, for the first time in her married life, had a proper kitchen. It was large and there was a wood-burning stove that was lit each morning in order to prepare breakfast for a family of ten. The bathroom and laundry-room were in the basement where the home help, or one of my sisters, did the family washing by hand. Again a stove was lit to heat the water for both the washing and bathing. As this was a laborious exercise, the younger children had to share a bath.

But the main attraction of the Schanzstrasse was that my father's youngest brother, Charles, had moved from Papa and lived just up the street from us with his wife and two children, Jacob and Lici.

All our neighbours were pleasant and likeable. The building

housed a second Jewish family – the Friedmans – and a Hungarian family – the Fehérs. In the street there was Mr Deutsch who ran a kosher grocery store up the road. The shop was near the local cinema. Nothing could keep us out of that cinema; every Sunday afternoon we went to see films starring Greta Garbo, Marlene Dietrich, Konrad Veidt and Erich von Stroheim.

In the basement of our home lived the German Hausmeister or concierge, Mr Hoffmann, who had a daughter called Eva, the first girl I ever kissed. Mr Hoffmann with his son, Heinrich, a mechanic, were continually tinkering with various mechanical inventions. As a child I was utterly absorbed by their projects and often used to join them to watch their work. The last project they worked on together was a perpetual mobilé – a machine that would generate its own movement. It was a scheme that was proving quite tricky and would end in disaster.

It was very early on a warm summer morning, not yet seven o'clock, when our household was awoken by the dull sound of an explosion beneath us. Munky and I scrambled to the headboard, next to the open window, and peered down into the street. Plumes of smoke came spiralling out of the basement.

Fritz, still pulling on his shirt, stuck his head around the door: 'Stay where you are.'

As soon as he disappeared, we moved to the door and could see mother and father in the hallway. Poking my head out of the window again, I reported to Munky that Fritz was coming out and entering the smoking basement doorway down below: 'What do you think has happened?'

'You can never tell with those two. Last week I saw them dragging in all sorts of things.'

'Like what?'

'All sorts. Metal and things. They are nuts about anything metal at the moment.'

Just then Fritz bounded back into the flat, grabbed the telephone and asked for an ambulance.

'What is happening?' I asked, entering the hallway in my nightshirt.

Fritz waved a hand at me to be quiet and spoke into the receiver. Heinrich had been injured. And from what we could gather, quite badly. Mother shepherded Munky and me back to our room. 'Don't ask so many questions. Go, get dressed and stay in your room.'

With the bedroom door firmly shut behind us, we leapt back onto the bed and searched for signs of activity on the street, speculating about Heinrich's injuries.

About twenty minutes later a white van arrived and two men disappeared into the basement. They returned moments later, supporting Heinrich who clutched a towel to his bloody face. Later we learned that he had lost an eye in the explosion. Munky had been right about their recent passion for scrap metal. Heinrich had found an old grenade and when he attempted to dismantle it, the trigger mechanism had gone off.

Apart from that incident, the Schanzstrasse was a peaceful street. As well as the cinema and the grocer, there was Kraijchirovich, the barber, whose shop was straight across the street from our house. Mr Kraijchirovich was a tall, middle-aged German gentleman who sported a moustache. Once a month we would sit in one of his high swivel chairs while he, in his white coat, looking like a distinguished and learned professor, would trim our hair and ask about the rest of the family. He would often make jokes about school.

This affluent and tranquil period of our lives was relatively short-lived, partly because of father's poor business acumen and partly because he was totally oblivious to the ramifications of his generosity.

We were considered a well-to-do family (mainly because my father enjoyed spending his money) so we received a lot of guests. Often there were more than ten people sitting around the table at mealtimes. These included the usual relatives and friends, but father also brought home students or friends to talk to, and there was always a Bachur to feed (a poor student who attended the yeshivah, the Jewish religious college, but was fed and looked after by the Jewish community). The Bachurs ate their meals with a different family each day while continuing their studies.

My father was totally unaware of the extra strains such generosity put on both the household finances and my mother's catering skills. Many of his friends would turn up unannounced and adapting her cooking to accommodate the extra people required a certain degree of creativity. Mother could only do so much. We had to eat what we got. I did not complain – I liked everything. But the spontaneous arrival of guests meant that Munky and I (as we were the youngest) sometimes did not get our fair share. The working men and girls had to be fed first. We would have to make do with bread and whatever else was left over.

'Leopold, listen – you can't keep doing this to me,' I overheard my mother saying to my father one Friday after a particularly full house. 'Ernest and Alexander didn't get anything tonight.'

But father dismissed the subject: 'They will be all right. We'll make it up to them tomorrow.'

'Leopold, you've got a large family. You must put them first,' she continued. And father smiled at her and said, 'Mein Kind, don't worry – God will provide.' He never faced realities until it was too late – whether inside the house or on the streets outside.

~ • ~

Bratislava at that time was a city of diverse backgrounds – Slovakian, German, Jewish and Hungarian. In that area of the world you spoke several languages. My older brothers all knew German, Hungarian and Czech but, as a boy, I only spoke German. For the Germans Bratislava was called Pressburg, for the Hungarians it was Pozsony. It could have been a wonderful, rich and colourful place but underneath the cosmopolitan atmosphere the reality was very different. The Slovaks felt like underdogs in their own country, they were usually employed in menial labour or low-paid jobs in the service sector.

Generally, the German colony in Bratislava resented the formation of the Czechoslovak Republic. They were always looking back to the days of the Austro-Hungarian Empire where Germans had ruled over Slovaks, Czechs and other peoples. Many Germans had put their hopes on that other Austrian, Adolf Hitler, who had become Chancellor in Germany in 1933.

On the whole, the population of Bratislava was heavily influenced by what was happening in Nazi Germany. This added to the inevitable rivalries and prejudices between the different groups. From an early age we experienced anti-Semitism – whether it was just name-calling or the odd scuffle with German or Slovak children. This meant that my mother, or one of my older siblings, sometimes had to collect us from school or football matches if our journey came anywhere near the German quarter. To get home without being abused, molested or even beaten up began to be a daily challenge after 1933 when the German quarter started to become a no-go area for Jews.

Some children were quite crafty in catching you out. Often we turned a corner to find a small, innocent-looking girl standing in our path. 'Stinkende Juden!' the small child screamed at us – smelly Jews. A quick sweep of the horizon, revealing older children loitering menacingly near by, brought the realisation that the small one was trying to provoke a reaction. We knew better than to rise to the challenge, whatever abuse the youngster hurled at us. If you stood up for yourself then the whole gang descended upon you, 'defending' their younger comrade.

One day, coming back from a football match, Munky and I found ourselves face to face with a little girl yapping at us. A mob of about six boys were sitting on a nearby wall. We tried to ignore her but she persistently blocked our path; 'Don't ignore me, you filthy Jews.' Just then, mother turned the corner and heard the girl. She picked the girl up and gave her a good spanking across the bottom. The other children rapidly dispersed, deserting their accomplice. Mother was not going to have riff-raff like that treating her children in such a manner.

Therezia Hauser could take care of her family. She had come from a worldly Jewish family of cantors and rabbis who originated from Austria and Holland. Her mother, Antonia, came from one of the top Dutch-Jewish families. Her father's side of the family was from Vienna. Like my mother, many Jewish families in Bratislava had strong links with Vienna. The two cities were very close, both geographically and culturally.

My older brothers, Max, Fritz and Karl, often used to take the train into Vienna. Once away from their father's watchful eye, Max and Fritz especially, used Vienna as a hunting ground for girls. Max as the artistic bohemian dandy, always wearing long white cuffs to emphasise his long delicate hands, and Fritz dressed in his best pinstriped suit, were like two lady-killers on the loose. Of the two, Max was really spoiled. Father had first sent him for his business education to the Pfaff sewing-machine factory in Kaiserslautern but within a year he was dispatched to

Milan in order to learn singing. But not at an ordinary singing school; no, Max had to be taught by Benjamino Gigli – the Pavarotti of his day. Karl, in the meantime, studied at a conservatorium in Munich.

The trips to Vienna came to an end with the anschluss in 1938 – when Austria joined Hitler's Germany and mother's brother, Uncle Fritz, fled Vienna.

Uncle Fritz was an amazing individual – full of charm and humour. A Viennese theatrical comedian, he often performed sketches that Munky and I would imitate to amuse the family. They were tasteful, vaudeville sketches with real Viennese humour. We became very adept at performing one of his favourite skits: two grown men pretending to be babies in giant prams ridiculing the silly manner in which adults spoke to them. Inheriting Uncle Fritz's talent for mimicry, I soon became infamous for my impersonations of Mussolini and Hitler, whose images were becoming increasingly frequent on the newsreels at the local cinema.

Uncle Fritz was quite a character. He was a charmer and married at least six times. He even temporarily left the entertainment profession to become a rabbi, but managed to put his talents to equal use in both professions.

The Hauser theatrical genes filtered down into our family. Not only was I emerging as the comedian of the family, but my elder brother Max played both the violin and cello – often composing his own light classical pieces. When I was twelve he took me to hear a concert: Beethoven's Ninth, a piece about the coming of the Brotherhood of Men. Max could only afford the cheap seats behind the choir and as we were sitting there on the first row, I almost felt part of the choir and was so overwhelmed that I could not speak on the way home and was awake the whole night. He also took me to my first opera – Carmen.

In addition, my sisters were continually singing passages from operas and operettas – or contemporary songs made popular by Sara Leander or Marlene Dietrich. Their favourite song was a Neapolitan piece – 'Forget Me Not' – by Di Capua.

My brother Fritz had a wonderful bass voice which he used to sing Viennese operetta. But Karl preferred liturgical pieces. He was always the most serious minded and orthodox of the children, and later he became a cantor in the family tradition. He introduced me early in my musical education to singing cantorial music and started to show me how to use my voice properly.

The singing that would echo around the house became greatly enhanced by the purchase of a gramophone – at that time an expensive and prized possession. The windows were wide open from May till September and the music would cascade onto the Schanzstrasse. At times our whole life seemed to revolve around music and its beauty helped us to escape the harsh realities of life.

Father's side of the family was also talented. His father, Eliezer, and his grandfather before him, were all renowned cantors. My father had a great love for German lieder, Schubert and Mendelssohn, but coming from an orthodox family, cantorial music was his favourite. He served as honorary cantor of his synagogue in Bratislava.

But father's orthodoxy also meant that even though my sister Else had the most beautiful mezzo-soprano voice, it was only ever heard within the confines of our own home where the female family members were meant to stay until marriage.

This created tension for the girls, especially Lillie and Else. They were constantly compared with the lady-like Hedwig who was already contemplating settling down and was about to be engaged to a Jewish eye specialist.

Else was very beautiful, with the tiniest of waists. She wore whatever she could, within limits, to accentuate her curves and long legs. She was so attractive that at the age of sixteen, while still in braids, a respected Czech rabbi, fifty years old, approached the family with an unsuccessful offer of marriage.

While Else's dressing habits caused a lot of friction with my father, Lillie drove him to distraction. She was nice-looking too, but more independent and sensuous than Else. She was attracted to Bratislava's night life and the fast men who took her there. Father not only disapproved of her choice of men, clothing and the hours she kept, but he also did not appreciate her attitude. They used to have some terrible fights, and although he never hit her, he once did lay a finger on her when he tapped her on the shoulder with an outstretched forefinger after she had come home particularly late.

Not only the music, but also the orthodox religion made us oblivious to reality. There was no religious discussion in our house, only religious observance and dogma. At first my mother found the orthodox way of life difficult and alien to cope with. She had not wanted to marry a 'yeshivah boy', as she called father. Her god was of a pantheistic nature. As a child she had loved walking in the countryside with her family. Her own father, Mikhail Hauser, was still walking in his seventies, and that is how he passed away. One day he had reached the top of a hill and, sitting down, had peacefully died. So if my father headed off to the synagogue, mother would say, 'I can hear God's voice better when I go out into the hills – that's when I feel I am at one with God.'

Nevertheless, she was always prepared to listen to his side, even if she could not win the argument. Mother had the most beautiful and expressive large brown eyes. Traditionally women were never encouraged to talk much or have an opinion in an orthodox household. What their mouths could not express, their eyes made up for. During family discussions, usually dominated by my father, mother could express a whole world of commentary in her fleeting glances.

For her, the marriage was a matter of give and take. She had not wanted to marry an orthodox man, but she embraced the way of life and eventually came to enjoy its security and meaning. Because of the orthodox regulations, she had to wear a wig [sheitl] when she left the house. On the Sabbath the wig was also worn indoors. At all other times she would cover her head with a scarf.

If mother had compromised in her lifestyle, so too had my father. On cold winter nights mother would sit with her children in the kitchen in our house on the Schanzstrasse and tell stories about her brother Fritz, the rest of her family, her love of hill-walking and how my father had finally won her heart. She said he had seen her on the street one day and had brazenly gone up and introduced himself. She rejected his advances and continued to do so until, overwhelmed by his persistence, she replied that she would marry him if he let himself be educated by her: 'I want a husband I can be proud of and have respect for.'

Mother was especially fond of recounting how she had moulded her husband into the man he was. He had learned to be more worldly, even learning German – the language of the cultured and the enlightened – for her sake. And, despite becoming a housewife and mother of eight, she retained a pragmatic outlook on life. Mother and I shared the same scepticism. Once, after I had implied that father's dogmatic orthodoxy was naïve, she said: 'Keep it quiet. The world wants to be cheated. Let it be so.'

Father's side of the family, since before grandfather Eliezer, was firmly entrenched in the Jewish orthodox way of life. Father was a businessman – living in and dealing with the world – but he longed to be a religious philosopher at heart. He indulged in endless study of cabalistic philosophy and insisted that we went to religious classes every evening after ordinary school.

Initially I went to the Y'sodei Hatorah where we studied the Torah. It was a very strict school with the teacher walking up and down the rows of desks with a cane in his hand. You could be punished for the most minor transgression. On Saturday mornings, instead of having the day off like Christian children, we had to attend the shul [synagogue] classes for a further four hours. If you were unlucky, you had to sit a viva. If your father happened to turn up on a Saturday morning, you could bet your life that it would be your turn for an oral test. And it could be on any subject. There was no warning, nothing. The worst thing a pupil could do was to humiliate his father in public by giving a bad viva. I suffered, especially as I was living in the shadow of Munky who made learning seem so easy.

If all that was not bad enough, we also had to go to a proper school where we were taught the usual subjects: reading, writing, arithmetic, history and so on. Having studied all day we were hardly alert enough to take in our religious education. The Y'sodei Hatorah was preparation for the yeshivah. My older brothers had been sent to a well-known yeshivah in Galanta – not far from Bratislava.

Leopold Löwy wanted his sons to be religious philosophers, not businessmen like himself. Karl was a brilliant Talmudic scholar who became a dux at the Galanta Yeshivah. This meant he was allowed to escort the rabbi to Marienbad on holy days. When Karl eventually left for Munich in 1936 to become a cantor, my father could relax – at least one of his sons was well on the way to becoming a religious leader. As this all happened before the place of my secondary education was chosen, I merely went to the local yeshivah – the Yeshivah K'Tana.

Not only did father badly prepare us for the real world, but he also fooled himself. During the late 1930s his earnings began to decrease and he did not realise how steeply the family finances were declining until it was too late.

At first it appeared that business was continuing to do well. In 1935 we could afford to take over a second flat in the house when the Féhers moved out. This was a luxurious flat with its own bathroom. My father used the flat to entertain his boss and other business clients. For the children it was a forbidden area. But it meant that we could now have the run of our original flat.

After Karl's departure in 1936, father persisted in maintaining the family unity and that nearly ruined his business. When Max and Fritz came of age, my father decided to take them into the firm to help him run it, if only to keep them in Bratislava. Someone had to go to make room for my brothers and that person was Mr Weiss, the accountant. An important part of the business's success, however, depended on the abilities of the accountant, and none of my older brothers had the slightest interest in accountancy or managerial ability – when not chasing girls they were more interested in music or religious debate – so the agency suffered greatly after Mr Weiss had been fired.

None of us were aware of how bad the situation was until one day my mother ran into our bedroom carrying an armful of her jewellery and other precious objects. 'Here, get your coats on,' she told Munky and me. 'Put these in your pockets and go for a walk. Don't come back till after lunchtime.'

Confused, we did as we were instructed, and slipped on our

coats. As we walked down the front hall we saw our father in the dining-room in the company of a very serious-looking gentleman. Neither of them noticed us as we scooted out of the door with mother closing it quietly after us.

It was a hot summer day but neither Munky or myself dared remove our coats as we wandered out into the countryside. When we returned the serious-looking gentleman was gone but father looked exhausted. Mother retrieved her jewels from our pockets and we sat down to lunch.

The stranger had been the tax inspector. Father had not kept up his payments when the business started to go into decline. Still, he refused to do something pragmatic to salvage the situation. Later that day I heard mother quietly arguing with him about the morning's events. 'Don't worry,' he assured her in the usual manner. 'God will look after us and the children.'

My father failed to see that the world was changing. At home the praying, singing, music and laughter went on. Most of the Jewish families we knew were deluding themselves. They expected that the storm-clouds would disappear – as had happened before in Jewish history. Instead, they placed false hopes in the coming of the Messiah and fruitless prayer. This diverted people from taking rational action before it was too late.

Mother may have realised this and so did Leopold's brother Charles.

~ • ~

Charles Löwy was also a businessman, but he was not strictly orthodox. For instance, he did not insist on his wife wearing a sheitl or a scarf. He was also familiar with the people who went to the Mizrachi, a religious Zionist organisation. Zionism, the wish to resettle in Palestine, was a forbidden subject among orthodox Jews like my father. To the orthodox, to migrate to the Holy Land meant to bypass God's promise that only He could lead His people there after the arrival of the Messiah. So they were waiting for Him.

Charles decided not to wait. One morning in 1937 our house awoke to sounds of hammering and movement across the street in Charles's house. Hedwig and mother were in the process of lighting the stove to cook breakfast. Max came in with an armload of wood.

'What a racket,' he winced.

My father ignored this at first but eventually put down his book and stuck his head out the window to have a look. He then beckoned to me.

'Ernest, go and see what your Uncle Charles is up to.'

I ran across the street and poked my head inside Charles's door to see a couple of men nailing up wooden crates just as my cousin Jacob jumped down the stairs.

'Yankel, what's happening?' I asked.

'We're off to Palestine. Isn't it great?' he replied.

'Palestine,' I repeated. That word had been mentioned by Uncle Charles during one of his discussions with father, but was subsequently declared taboo in our household.

'We thought you were just joking,' I stammered. Talking about Palestine was one thing, but to leave everything here was inconceivable.

Just then Uncle Charles's tall frame hove into view. 'That's right, we're off,' he said. 'Your father wouldn't believe me. You'd better go and tell him it's true.'

'What?' thundered my father over the breakfast table, making all the other children jump in surprise. 'I don't believe it. I can see I'll have to go there and sort this out.'

Mother was nonplussed. Wiping her hands on her apron she said, 'I knew it.' And then more meaningfully to father she added, 'And you know what? I've got a strong feeling that he's right.'

My father ignored her comment and, jumping up from his chair, tore across the road. Mother and I exchanged glances. Shrugging her shoulders she said, 'Come, let's eat. I think your father will be quite some time.'

Charles did not listen to my father and set off for Palestine as planned with his family.

~ • ~

A year later, when I was thirteen, Uncle Charles came back for a brief visit. He looked tanned, happy and healthy. We were all very curious to hear about Palestine but were too timid to ask questions in front of father. After the family meal I heard my father arguing with him in private. Much later, in Batyam, near Tel Aviv, Charles recounted the conversation to me.

'Leopold, how can you just sit here and hope that everything will be all right?' he had asked. 'Can't you see that you are sitting on a time-bomb here? The Nazis are only forty miles away!'

'Since when does anything change?' my father retorted wearily. 'This Nazi business is just like all the other inflictions we Jews have had to endure. It's nothing new.'

'This is different,' Charles insisted. 'The Nazis mean business. How would Noah have survived if he had not built his ark? Can't you see that the Nazi flood is rising everywhere?'

'It'll all blow over. Like a bad thunderstorm. There was no need to go running off to Palestine.'

'Palestine is the only alternative.'

'Palestine is for God to give,' Father shouted angrily. 'You, a pioneer – a Zionist! How could you? Only God can return us to the Holy Land. You ought to be ashamed.'

'Leopold, wake up – look around and see what's happening. You may prefer to put your faith in the Torah, but do you have the right to inflict the same decision on your entire family? Think of the children. Leopold, please, I'm asking for their sake – let me take some of them back to Palestine with me. Let them have a chance.'

'No! Never! Split up the family? Impossible. And I will not have you filling their heads with Zionist nonsense. It's because of your disobedience and that of those like you that God has sent the Nazis to punish us. I will not give up my faith like you.'

'But Leopold, I have not given up my faith . . .'

And so the argument had gone round in circles. My father would not budge from his orthodox position and Charles went back to Palestine empty handed. When 1937 became 1938 it was 'another new year, another Shabbat'.

Every day we continued to go to the Y'sodei Hatorah on the Turnergasse half an hour's walk away and we went to shul – another forty-five minutes' walk. The violence was increasing around us, but every day we had to take the risk of being beaten up because father had put his faith in blind orthodoxy. Mother had to come and collect us while father continued to bury himself among his books and his friends at the synagogue.

Father never explained what form the heavenly protection he spoke about would take. Munky was close to him in religious thought, but even he started to wonder about the alternatives, especially after a shattering incident with one of my friends – Helmut Palmer.

Helmut, who was about my age, lived across the road with his mother and was constantly in our house; he even came on holiday with us. But all of a sudden he joined the Hitler Youth and, coming up to the door in his new uniform one day, Helmut stated that he could no longer be my friend. He showed no sign of regret, no sense of loss. Maybe Uncle Charles had had the right idea.

'Another family is leaving for Palestine: one of their boys is in my class – they're off next Monday,' said Munky one day over homework.

'Really? Must be nice to live in a place where there are only Jews.'

'Oh, there are Arabs as well – quite a few. There've been a few fights.'

'How do you know?'

'Yankel told me. He used to go to the Mizrachi shul, remember?' He paused and then continued: 'Strange that his shul's in the same building as ours, they even use the same door . . .' He smiled at me meaningfully.

I began to get the picture.

'Like no one would really see if we'd been in one shul or the other,' I ventured.

Then Munky looked at me seriously and said hurriedly in a quiet voice, 'We mustn't tell anyone though. Can you imagine what would happen if father found out?'

'I don't know what's worse,' I quipped, 'getting a beating at home for wanting to go to Palestine or staying in Bratislava and getting a beating by the Slovak mob.'

When we arrived at the Mizrachi shul it was full. Pictures and photographs of Palestine adorned the walls and we were made to feel very welcome, especially by the other young people. One of the speakers was only sixteen or seventeen years old. His name was Emil Zimet. He spoke with passion about Palestine being the only viable alternative for Jewish life in an increasingly hostile world. Neither Jewish assimilation nor Jewish self-segregation had worked, he argued. Afterwards it was wonderful to be able to have an open discussion with the others.

We went back a couple of times. The last time we attended Emil told us that the Mizrachi were organising a retreat for two weeks. We would be able to go camping with the others and follow up on our discussions, learning more about Palestine. Munky was extremely enthusiastic. There was only one problem. How on earth could we broach the subject with father?

The matter resolved itself the following week when my father was summoned to Y'Sodei Hatorah shul.

'Do you know what your two boys have been up to?' the teacher demanded of my father. 'You will not believe it!' he continued. Father blinked his eyes wondering what heinous crime we had committed. 'They went to the Mizrachi shul for their prayers.'

Someone had spotted us and reported back. Father was dumbfounded.

'What are you going to do about it?' demanded the teacher, slamming his cane across the table.

Needless to say, when we got home my father was furious.

Mother looked at us sympathetically as he thundered on dogmatically: 'Palestine is for God to give. Become a Zionist and you break the faith.'

How could he have been so blind? All around us anti-Semitism was on the rise. In 1938 the Nazis were just across the border in Vienna and the Slovakian authorities were looking more favourably towards Hitler. Jews, like Uncle Fritz who had fled from Austria, came with stories of violence and unleashed hatred. The whole situation engendered an oppressive atmosphere both at home and in the synagogue.

I was now thirteen. It was time for my Bar Mitzvah – traditionally a joyous occasion with lots of singing and customarily a huge family party. But everyone's mind was distracted by the political situation. Not much attention was paid to the forthcoming Bar Mitzvah. There was no planning. And on the day of the service the mood among the congregation was one of gloom. Moreover, there was no traditional party. No one could force themselves into a celebratory mood. For me, the only respite from the increasing tension and my father's religious zeal was football.

On the whole, the Jewish population of Bratislava kept apart from the other population groups but sometimes there were sports events where people mingled. Our district had a good Jewish football team made up from boys of all ages, including Munky and me. We used to play on the empty grounds around our houses. The footballs were made from pieces of newspaper made damp and stuck together like papier mâché and then tied up with string for good measure. We played in our ordinary clothes and, except for a few of us, we had no proper boots. When someone with football boots went for the ball at the same time as you, the collision could do you some serious damage.

Most districts or streets had their own team and there was a kind of league in Bratislava which had been organised by the older boys. In our team it was the responsibility of Kalman Hilvert and Egon Reisman to negotiate fixtures with other groups. League matches were played on a real football field with goalposts and even a genuine leather ball.

Towards the end of 1938 we were scheduled to play against the team of the neighbouring German quarter. This was practically adjacent to the Schanzstrasse. It began just off our street on a road called the Zehnhaüser and it was strictly forbidden territory.

The German boys came to hover about the Schanzstrasse as we kicked the ball about and taunt us. Their jeers only made us more determined to beat them at a proper game and so Kalman and Egon set up a match – in the German quarter.

Other Jewish boys said that we were mad. 'You'll get pummelled,' my brother Max warned me. 'You'd better not let Fritz find out or he'll just lock you in the house.'

Fritz, even though he was only the third eldest son, had begun to take on many of the responsibilities usually associated with a father's role. Mother and father would rarely punish us. Fritz was in charge of discipline and usually had to mete out the various punishments.

Despite the spectre of Fritz, we strode boldly into the German quarter to meet our fate. As soon as we arrived on the pitch we knew this game had no pretence of being a 'friendly'. The German squad cruised onto the field in full kit – black and white striped tops and shorts (the colours of the German national team). More importantly, they all had football boots. Munky and I glanced down at our scuffed and extremely ordinary shoes. 'We're going to get hammered,' I said.

'We'd better give them a reason, then,' muttered Munky and sauntered onto the pitch.

If the appearance of the German footballers was not bad enough, it soon became clear that the spectators were just as dangerous. All Germans, parents and friends, they had nothing but contempt for us.

Munky was undeterred and within the first thirty minutes he had scored a goal. It was nearing half-time and when the score shot up to 2-0, the first anti-Semitic comments rained down on us like missiles. Most of the German tackling became somewhat questionable and Kalman gathered us together for a quick confab.

'If I give the signal, we just go. Have a quick look. There are four exits. The best plan is to split up. If you think you can scale that wall over there, you're almost back in the Czech quarter.'

The aggressive tackling continued unabated and the spectators began to move closer to the touch-lines. It did not help matters much when Munky scored a beautiful third goal. A stone was thrown and the opposition did not even try to pretend they were tackling any more. All our eyes were on Kalman who wisely gave the signal and we were off.

With Munky hot on my heels, I pelted out of one of the exits and down the street. I did not look round for fear. When I reached the corner of the Schöndorferstrasse a tram came by and I managed to swing myself onto the carriage.

Catching my breath and finally looking behind me, I could see no sign of Munky. Later that evening he returned to the house covered in cuts and bruises. They had given him quite a beating. Mother and Father did not say a word. Even Fritz could not be angry with us when he saw Munky's face. When Munky tried to explain our reasons for taking part in the match – that it was a matter of honour – my father looked at us and said, 'It doesn't matter what other people think or do. Don't you get involved. You shouldn't get carried away with all this nonsense. Just be yourself. Never mind what anyone else is doing.'

The paradox was that Father was as right as he was wrong. It was important to be true to yourself and not get caught up in petty political rivalries but there were moments when reality had to be faced and decisions had to be made. However, there was no arguing with Father. But, still, his unquestioning creed was shattered soon, albeit briefly, when one bright Saturday morning he too became the object of the escalating violence.

My brothers and I had returned from the synagogue, leaving father outside talking with one of his friends. Munky and I had run home with Max and Fritz ambling behind us. Time wore on, it was nearly lunchtime, and still there was no sign of Father. 'Probably yapping on with one of those yeshivah students again,' sighed my mother. But still he did not return.

Then suddenly the front door slowly swung open and my father shuffled in. A large bloody gash was gouged in his forehead and his Shabbat clothes were ripped and dirty. His right arm hung lifelessly against his side. He was a small man – but now he looked even smaller. He had worn a brave face when he had entered but, seeing the horrified expressions on our faces, he simply burst into tears. I had never seen him break down like that before and I could not help crying myself.

He had left his friend on the street and was coming back via an alley onto the Schanzstrasse when he had been attacked by three or four teenage boys – German or possibly Slovakian. They had pushed him to the ground and broken his right shoulder bone and then, after kicking him as he lay on the ground, ran off. They had not stolen a thing.

'I can hear the alarm bells ringing,' he warned my mother as he choked back the tears and she cleaned his forehead with a damp towel. 'We must get out of here. We must leave Czechoslovakia at once. There is no future here.'

Max, Fritz and the girls looked perturbed. Leave home? Mother and I exchanged looks of doubt at father's sudden change of heart.

Sure enough, when he returned from hospital with his arm in a sling and we sat down to our Sabbath meal, father refused to discuss the subject again. 'I won't let it spoil my Sabbath,' he forcefully announced. It was as if the attack had never happened and we were not going to leave Bratislava. We had a lovely meal, singing all the traditional table songs. The grace was said after the meal and we all had our customary afternoon nap. The subject was never broached again.

For years it had gone on: 'One more New Year, one more Holy Day, one more Sabbath.' Father's attitude was, 'The Nazi madness will pass.' It was just like a well-known Hungarian folk-song by Zoltan Kodály: a little girl repeatedly pleads with her mother to leave the tavern to go home to see her husband who is very ill. But the woman is enjoying herself and refuses. Every time the child begs her to come home, the mother replies that she will come after 'just one more dance'. The final time the girl returns to the tavern is to tell her mother that the father has died. During the 1920s and 1930s there were many in Bratislava who suffered from the 'just one more dance' syndrome – refusing to face reality and make decisions until it was too late.

It was an attitude that was ingrained through religious instruction. In the orthodox Jewish community many sought refuge from hardship and persecution in their hopes about the coming of the Messiah, rather than doing something themselves. The Jewish faith has a long history of interpreting victimisation as the mere birth-pangs of the Messiah – the greater the suffering, the closer He is at hand. Many, including my father, were adherents of this philosophy. They put their heads in the sand and refused to see the reality. To every question mother put forward, my father waved his hand and said, 'Mein Kind, God will help us. He will provide.' And then he buried his head again in books such as *The Duties of the Heart* – an ancient exposition on ethical and moral aspects which was his favourite religious book.

However, it was not long before our departure from Czechoslovakia was decided for us. On the evening of 4

November 1938, news started spreading during the synagogue service about parts of the Slovakian highlands being annexed by the Hungarian dictator Horthy, following a bargain he had made with Hitler. In the atmosphere of those days this could only lead to repercussions for people with Hungarian backgrounds which would affect us directly. Although father had been living and working for years in Czechoslovakia, he had never applied for Czech citizenship and still held his Hungarian nationality.

It was a long walk home that night from the synagogue. It began to rain. When we arrived home, no one had much of an appetite, despite the wonderful meal my mother and sisters had cooked. Father was not very talkative and Fritz told mother about the news. No one sang that evening; silence entombed the house and the meal seemed to have been forgotten. It got later and later and the noises in my stomach got louder and louder. Eventually, I tugged on my father's sleeve as he sat in thought in his chair and gestured at the table. It was nearly eight o'clock and I was famished.

'All right,' he said, rousing himself and slapped his hands together. 'Let's eat.' But as the house burst into movement and life again, we did not hear buses drawing up on the street outside. Father was standing up, about to recite the Kiddush, and had placed the goblet of wine back on the table when the sound of a knock on the door suddenly pierced our forced joviality. We froze. Mother straightened up and automatically drew Lillie, the youngest girl, close to her. Father stood there, not knowing what to do. The second rap sounded even more ominous.

'I'll get it,' said Fritz, looking at my father and he moved to the door. Father hovered behind his son and I sneaked up behind both of them in the corridor.

Fritz opened the door and, without waiting to be invited in, two men brusquely entered. The first was a small man in civilian clothes who shook the rain off his coat in a slapdash manner. The second, dawdling behind him, was a Slovakian policeman.

'Leopold Löwy?' asked the first man in Czech with a strong German accent, staring menacingly at Fritz.

'I am Leopold Löwy,' said my father, straightening up.

The German eyed him coldly; 'You have ten minutes to pack. You are leaving Czechoslovakia. There are buses waiting below.'

We stood there not quite knowing what to do.

'Ten minutes,' the German emphasised again. 'Don't keep me waiting.'

We offered no resistance. Fatalistically resigned to our destiny, stricken by fear and anxious not to worsen the situation, we were incapable of acting. No one spoke a word, except the odd instruction about what to take. Mother helped the girls to pack, the German keeping a firm eye on them, even following my sister Else when she had to go to the toilet. The Slovakian policeman looked embarrassed and offered to help carry things down for us.

'Make sure you pack some food,' he told us in a low voice. 'And wear something warm.'

Mother made up little bundles of bread and cheese before she took the younger children, including me, to one of the four or five red buses that were waiting on the Schanzstrasse. The rain was quite heavy and by now there was an icy wind blowing. The buses were already fairly full of other families. We stumbled onto the vehicle in a daze. Sitting there I looked up at the house. The lights were still on and I thought of the dinner still sitting in the oven. There was no music to be heard, the time of dancing was over.

2

KRAIJCHIROVICH IS
SMILING

~

The last one to enter the dark bus on the Schanzstrasse was father. He had come running down the steps just as the police started to board up and seal the house. We could see him through the window of the bus. He seemed to stop, hesitate momentarily in the rain and stare across the road. I craned my neck to see what it was he was so engrossed with. When he got on the bus he was shaking. Tears were running down his face, mingling with the streaks of rain: 'You won't believe this,' he said to mother, his voice trembling, 'but Kraijchirovich is standing in the doorway of his shop – smiling. The man is actually smiling.'

Kraijchirovich, the German barber who had cut our hair and made jokes about school, was glad to see us leave. We had provided him with some of his best custom but he must have always envied us, having to listen to the music and laughter coming from our windows.

~

The reaction from the barber showed us that even those who were not openly hostile, those we had believed to be our friends, had secretly longed for our removal from their street. Year after year the hatred had built up. The Hungarian government was responsible for their troops occupying Slovakian land, and although Hitler was to blame, our neighbours took their revenge on the Jews. The buses in the Schanzstrasse contained only Jewish families; the barber's smile announced that for Jews the party was over.

Father's mistake was that he had never applied for Czech citizenship. Now, once again, he seemed resigned to our fate. He was not alone, about a hundred families from our district walked peaceably onto the buses. Where we were being driven to, no one knew.

We drove past the outskirts of Bratislava into the dark countryside along uneven dirt-tracks. The rain turned into a dense sleet that intermittently cracked against the windows with the force of the wind. Through them, only the impenetrable black of night showed. Not a soul. Not a light.

It must have been after midnight when the bus suddenly stopped. The headlights revealed nothing of our location. Quickly the doors opened and we were ordered off. As we alighted we sank ankle-deep into oozing mud and found ourselves in a barren and unwelcoming countryside. A desolate place: no trees to offer shelter, the indifferent sleet hammered against our faces. Then, without explanation, the bus's doors suddenly shut, the vehicle turned round and left us standing there.

'Where are we?' asked Max, shielding his eyes against the ice and scanning the horizon through narrowed eyes.

'I think we must be at the border with Hungary,' said Fritz.

'We're in no man's land,' a stranger next to us explained.

'"Hungarians, go back to Hungary," that's what one of their policemen told us.'

People just stood there not knowing what to do, except to put their backs against the rain like horses do in the fields. Some sat down on their suitcases. Young people tried to protect their elders, while parents endeavoured to shelter their children by using their bodies as armour against the elements. Mother and Else tried to shield my sister Hedwig as much as possible. Hedwig had been sickly ever since her fiancé, the Jewish eye specialist, had died of cancer the year before. She had only just recovered from pneumonia and would not last long in this downpour.

'What's that then?' asked Max pointing to a small light flickering on the horizon.

'A farm?' suggested Munky.

'Whatever it is, or whoever lives there – perhaps they can tell us how to get to the nearest town,' said Fritz. 'Who's coming?'

The girls stayed to look after our parents and Hedwig. Max, Munky, myself and some of the other men and boys set off following Fritz. We battled against the sleet all the way, fighting against it like the current of a river, towards our only hope twinkling unwittingly on the horizon.

We were lucky. The distant light we had spotted was a house on the outskirts of the Hungarian border village of Kisabony. Fritz knocked on the first door we came to and explained to the stunned people inside what had happened in Bratislava. The word went out and the inhabitants, many of whom had already gone to bed, got up and opened their doors to us. If Kraijchirovich had shaken our faith in human nature, then the human solidarity we witnessed in Kisabony reaffirmed it. Rebuilding fires that had only just been put out for the night, total strangers heated milk for the young ones and prepared food for others. Many went out into the rain heading for the no man's land where my parents waited with the sick and elderly. Most of us took shelter in a little synagogue after we had been given something to warm our stomachs and that is where we fell asleep.

I awoke to the smell of extinguished candles mingling with the odour of old books and the sweet scent of a smouldering log fire. Opening my eyes, I noticed that Fritz had disappeared. The first traces of daylight filtered through the windows. My companions were people of all ages and classes. Many were already awake but were shivering and they lacked the energy to move. After the rapid events of the previous night a feeling of lethargic hopelessness had taken hold of us.

This changed when Fritz returned and gathered together some of the men. He explained there was a larger village nearby called Dunajszka Streda. He had been told that it had a large Jewish population and that we might receive more help there. Moreover, Dunajszka Streda had a railway station which would enable people to travel to friends and relatives who were further afield.

About twenty of us set off on foot, our clothes still damp from the night before. Dunajszka Streda turned out to be a good ten kilometres away. It was bitterly cold and the bottoms of our still-sopping trousers flapped around our ankles. When we arrived, a group of men and boys were just on their way to the synagogue for the Saturday service. They stopped as we approached up the road. We must have been a suspicious and sorry-looking lot.

Fritz once again took the initiative and headed towards the strangers: 'We are Jews from Bratislava. We have been expelled.'

Amongst these Hungarian Jews who listened gravely to Fritz

as he continued with the story of our plight was an older man. 'Come with me,' he said suddenly and shepherded us towards the nearby synagogue. We timidly followed his striding figure through an oak door. The men inside fell silent in mid-prayer, staring at us, astounded.

We quickly realised that our newly found patron was the senior warden of the community. Explaining who we were and what fate had befallen Bratislava Jewry, he made a passionate appeal to his people to take us into their homes. Like Kisabony, Dunajszka Streda burst into a flurry of activity. Even though it was the Sabbath, the rabbi ordered that normal Sabbath regulations forbidding travel and work should be broken and that horses and carts be sent back to Kisabony to collect the rest of us.

A well-dressed and good-looking young man dashed out muttering to a friend, 'You take the other one.' He handed him a set of keys. Looking out of the synagogue window, it was not long before I saw the two men again as they drove past in two immaculate-looking cars — one of which was a Tatra, a very expensive and comfortable model.

So it was in Dunajszka Streda, in the middle of turmoil and tragedy, that two love affairs occurred.

The handsome car owner returned to town with my mother and sisters. And it was Else who was sitting up front with this dashing stranger. The gentleman, Bernat Rujder, immediately escorted my sisters to his own home where he put them up. In a matter of no time at all he fell in love with Else. My sister had certainly landed on her feet. Having lost everything in Bratislava, she was now being welcomed into a considerably wealthy family. But more important than that, Bernat proved to be an extremely charming, generous and virtuous individual who always put others before himself.

In the meantime, mother and I lodged with the Weiss family, a well-to-do couple with three children – two girls, Lici, aged eleven, Medy, aged thirteen, and a boy, Ernö, of sixteen. There we enjoyed the comfort of a friendly and warm household. After the last 24 hours we could finally relax and take stock of our situation.

Many people visited the Weiss household to learn what had happened to the refugees from Bratislava. Among them were family friends and total strangers, for instance a Mr Spiegel who always listened patiently to our stories and tried to reassure us that now we would be safe.

However, I was further to be diverted from the concerns of my family's immediate problems by the Weiss's eldest daughter, Medy. As soon as I walked into the Weiss's home my heart jumped at the sight of her. With her big blue eyes and her soft, long brown hair falling down about her shoulders, she was instantly beguiling. From then on she would never be out of my mind.

I picked an awkward moment, but I was in love. And this was more serious than ever before. Whenever I saw Medy, my knees went weak. I watched her, fascinated, as she moved gracefully about the house. That first Saturday afternoon we played a game of cards over a small table and my knee touched hers. The sensation went through my body like an electric shock. She alone occupied the centre of my existence and represented the nearest thing to a heavenly phenomenon. I was overtaken by the irresistible desire to be continually in her company.

I was hardly fourteen. Living with my secret love was comforting after what we had just been through but at the same time the situation was very difficult. It was the week of the annexation of the Slovakian highlands. In the street Medy and I watched the endless stream of Hungarian occupation troops sitting triumphantly on their shaky horse-drawn carriages with their outdated armoury, jolting from side to side on the cobbled stones. I paid more attention to Medy standing close to me than to the parade itself.

She must have sensed my feelings for her, but our strict religious upbringing dictated that she should never acknowledge them. And I could never declare my emotions openly. However, love found a way.

'He sings?' repeated Mrs Weiss, replacing her cup on the table. It was true enough, I had been singing in the synagogue choir since the age of five and was known for my outstanding soprano voice.

'Yes, our Ernest has a good voice,' said my mother. 'Don't you?'

I was staring at Medy across the living-room.

'Why don't you sing for us now? . . . Ernest?' I started to regain composure at the repetition of my name.

'Now?' I muttered, realising that I had gone bright red.

'I'd love to hear you sing,' Medy's mother said.

Sheepishly I stood up and began – shakily at first but then growing in confidence as I saw Medy's face enraptured.

Singing, I discovered, provided me with a way to pour out my tormented heart to her. I was often asked to perform for the Weiss family after that – especially when they had guests like Mr Spiegel. Unaware of the source of my passion, these performances often forced my audience to search for their handkerchiefs.

We were in the Weiss household for only a week but, because of Medy's presence, it seemed timeless. However, we were merely guests and eventually had to move on.

Our family was split up in an effort to find temporary accommodation and work for all of us. Distant family members had often visited the 'golden calf' on the Schanzstrasse where they had received abundant hospitality. Now it was father's turn to receive a little of that same generosity in return. But a family of ten was difficult to accommodate. It would have been impossible to stay together at that time. So it was decided that I should go alone to my grandfather who lived in Papa.

It was early on a Sunday morning when we gave our thanks and said farewell to our hosts. I noticed that the door to the girls' bedroom was open. I sneaked in. The younger sister had just woken and was sitting up in bed. She watched with amazement as I went over to the still-sleeping Medy and gently touched her hand. As she awoke I pressed her fingers to my lips, she did not say a word. Hearing mother call for me, I quickly slipped out of the room. Glancing back at Medy one last time, I wondered if I would ever see her again.

Munky and Else stayed in Dunajszka Streda, while Mother, Father and the others were to leave for the town of Komarom which was about a hundred kilometres from Papa. While my mother and sisters stood on one platform, my father put me on another train to grandfather's town. Mother waved from the other side of the station and tried to look brave. All I could think of was what an exciting adventure – to travel on my own. My exhilaration soon gave way to fatigue and discomfort as I discovered how long the journey was. The train had wooden benches to sit on and my body began to ache in no time at all. Not only that, but when I arrived at Papa station, I had no idea how to get to Grandfather's house and I began to feel very lost. I had visited Grandfather with the family a few times before, but now, on my own, everything looked unfamiliar. Luckily a station official saw me.

'I'm looking for my Grandfather. He lives in Papa,' I said in German.

'Yes, you looked a bit lost. That's quite a trek from here. And there are lots of grandfathers in this town, I'm afraid. Isn't anyone with you?'

'No, I came on my own.'

'Where are you from?' he asked. I told him about how the family had been expelled from Bratislava. He listened thoughtfully and then asked; 'What's your grandfather's name?'

'Eliezer,' I said. 'Eliezer Löwy.'

The station official smiled. 'So you're Elieizer Löwy's little grandson. I think I can help you find him.'

Luckily Grandfather was a well-known and respected member of his community.

Following the man's instructions I walked into town and located Grandfather's cottage. I knocked on the door. A tall, elderly man with a warm face and grey goatee beard opened the door. His deep, black eyes widened when he recognised his visitor. He was, needless to say, surprised to see me – little Ernest – standing there all on his own. He immediately bombarded me with questions: 'Moishe!' – he always called me Moishe – 'What on earth are you doing here? Where's Leopold?' then he stuck his head outside the door and looked up and down the street.

'It's just me, Grandfather.'

'All alone?' he said, taking me into the house. 'What happened? Is everyone all right? What about your mother? Your sisters?'

I told him. Grandfather turned away from me towards the window. He shook, started sobbing: the golden child of the family – Leopold Löwy – had lost his house and his fortune. He was as penniless as a peasant. All those years of hard work were wiped out in one night. He wiped away his tears, turned round, grinned at me and said, 'You must be hungry.' I grinned back. I was always hungry. He took me into the kitchen.

At that time the Jewish population of Papa numbered around 3,500. Grandfather Eliezer was their Oberkantor. Just walking by his side on the street made me feel proud and privileged. He had a natural air of dignity. It made passers-by, Jews and non-Jews, not only greet him with respect, but many accompanied their greeting with a discreet bow. For me he was one of the most wonderful human beings I have ever met – the embodiment of tolerance and understanding. He also had quite a sense of humour.

Eliezer's house, a one-storey, fairly spacious cottage, was in the grounds of the large synagogue where he held his position. The acoustics of the synagogue were extraordinary; when grandfather sang he sounded like a hundred bells – a deep, rich tenor voice like Caruso's. He could have sung opera, Wagner, anything would have sounded great. He soon realised that I too had a promising voice.

'You have a nice voice, you have a talent, let me give you the secret of correct singing.'

Taking me under his wing, he started to coach me. 'Never open your mouth too wide but keep everything around your mouth soft and relaxed.'

Not only did he imbue me with the skills I needed to project my voice, but also those I needed to protect it. He taught me many of his own favourite liturgical songs or what he called his 'party pieces', including one he had composed himself – 'Achenu Kol Beith Ysrael' – based on a spoken prayer for all Jewish people who suffer persecution. I still sing it today. Those days spent under grandfather's tuition were priceless. Moreover, I made my professional singing début while I was in Papa.

About ten days after my arrival, two other distant relatives turned up and with them was my father. At first I thought that he had come with the sole purpose of collecting me. But, like the other two relatives, he had been invited to a huge wedding. The rabbi's daughter was getting married. Hundreds upon hundreds of people were expected. It was to be the most important event in Papa's recent history.

How much I wanted to go, but my father told me it was impossible. 'We're getting up at the crack of dawn tomorrow,' he explained. 'We have to be at the station at five in the morning to catch the train to Budapest.' Father hoped to reunite the entire family there. 'You want to see the others again, don't you?'

'But I can sleep on the train,' I pleaded.

'On these wooden benches? Don't be silly.'

'But . . .'

'No buts, Ernest. Now go to bed.'

So, despite my appeals, I was left alone in the cottage while he and grandfather went off to the wedding with the other guests. I buried myself under my quilt, sulked and eventually dropped off to sleep.

At midnight I was woken up by my father throwing back this mound of quilts and bedclothes. 'Ernest, get up. Grandfather says you must come.' And he flung some clothes at me.

'Come where?' I yawned incoherently.

'You've got to come to the wedding.'

'I don't want to go any more,' I was still sulking.

'Don't argue,' bellowed my father, forcing one of my arms down a shirtsleeve. 'If Grandfather says you've got to come, you've got to come. His word is sacrosanct.'

He quickly finished dressing me and then half-dragged me, half-carried me along the dark streets of Papa until we arrived at a large hall where the wedding reception was taking place.

When grandfather saw me, he hauled me over to the centre of the hall and, sweeping the crockery and glasses aside from a large table, picked me up and placed me on it. I was still half-asleep. He seized a glass of wine and thrust it into my hands. 'Drink,' he commanded. I gulped the wine down and wiped the sleep from my eyes.

'Moishe, listen to me. Now remember what I told you about singing? Remember that piece I taught you yesterday?' I nodded but did not really understand. 'Well, sing it now.'

I stared into the unknown faces of hundreds of wedding guests. They were laughing and shouting. Women were running about carrying trays loaded down with gateaux and sweetmeats; chocolate cake, fudge cake, cream cake, fruit cake. It was heaven. 'Sing!' grandfather repeated. I stared at the cake. 'Sing and you can have your cake later.'

I sang all night. I sang liturgical pieces. I sang grandfather's own compositions. I put my whole heart into it. Grandfather stood in front of me, like a singing master, thumping the table and telling me which piece to sing next. The guests were delighted and called out for more. It was my first public singing performance and I was a hit. Grandfather stood in front of me, proud of his little grandson.

Eventually I was carried off back to grandfather's cottage, grasping a fistful of cake. No sooner had I laid my head on the pillow than it was dawn and father was throwing my clothes at me again. After the wine, the lack of sleep and all that singing, the fumes from the cheap Hungarian cigarettes people were smoking at Papa train station left me feeling sick to my stomach. My father and I boarded the morning train to Budapest and again I had to endure the hard wooden benches. Father was right; the idea of trying to get some sleep on those seats was farcical.

At the train station we caught a tram. Our first mission was to find accommodation. Descending from the tram on one side of the main streets, we were met by a group of about five hundred people protesting, 'The Jews are too rich; the Jews have too much power in the workplace; the Jews are taking over the universities.' That was our welcome to the Hungarian capital and the mood engendered in late 1938. It appeared that our new neighbours were not so much different from those in Bratislava.

My father managed to rent a one-room flat in the Jewish quarter. It was all he could manage by scraping together all his money. The flat was sparsely furnished and had no kitchen or cooking area. At first the landlady thought she was just leasing the flat to a man and his son. But when more members of the family arrived, she did not give us any trouble and was very sympathetic to our plight. There was one double bed which some of the family slept in – widthways – while the rest slept on the floor and in armchairs.

Karl was the first to arrive. My father found him quite by accident. One Friday night in the Kazinczy synagogue in Budapest an old business acquaintance came up to my father saying, 'Herr Löwy, I see Karl has got here safely then.'

'What?' said my father, looking at him somewhat bemused.

'That was Karl I saw, wasn't it? Outside, on the street just now?'

Without another word, my father darted out of the synagogue to scour the streets. When he found his son it was an emotional reunion. Karl had not even known that the family had been expelled from Bratislava. He had come to Budapest from Munich after the Kristallnacht, narrowly escaping the SS. On the evening of the Kristallnacht, 9 November 1938, Karl had gone to his rabbi's apartment to say goodbye, having decided to leave Germany. As he mounted the staircase he heard a commotion above him. The rabbi was in the process of being arrested. The Nazis hurriedly swept down the stairs before Karl had a chance to think. Luckily, he had his Hungarian passport in his pocket. That piece of paper saved his life.

Still, Karl was a sensitive, quiet man and all the recent stress had caused internal stomach bleeding. He had arrived in Budapest in a poor state. Neither he nor us knew about the bleeding and he was taken into hospital where his condition was eventually diagnosed. The prognosis was not hopeful, as he had lost a lot of blood.

At that point Max arrived unannounced in Budapest, just in the nick of time. A transfusion of blood from Max saved Karl's life. A short while later my mother and the rest of the family came from Komarom. Else, however, was perfectly happy to stay in Dunajszka Streda with Bernat. She had packed Munky off on the train so that she could be alone with her future husband.

All our belongings and investments had been abandoned in Bratislava. The family had to start again from scratch. Life was difficult: days were long, the pay was insufficient. The family income left little over for buying new clothes. We had not brought heavy coats with us, and so the first winters in Budapest were hard. Father's shoulder played up in the cold as it had never properly mended after the attack in Bratislava. At first he picked up a job as an agent for a bag manufacturer — selling their merchandise to retail stores. But it was not enough for the family to live on and so he acquired a second agency selling sheets and towels.

Having reached an age when you were expected to learn a trade, I started work to contribute to the family finances. I went to work in a light-engineering workshop where brass pipes were manufactured for the gas-works. The workshop was located in the basement of a building in one of Budapest's red-light districts and, looking from my workbench, I could see the clattering heels through the window. Being an apprentice I had to open up the place each morning. At night I had to stay behind and sweep the floor, collecting little scrap pieces of brass that had ended up on the floor. Every bit of brass had to be saved and recycled.

But I was only fourteen and small for my age. The work was too heavy and the hours too long. It was bitterly cold that winter and I did not have enough warm clothes to protect me. My health started to suffer. After eight months my father managed to get me a new job in a fountain-pen workshop run by a Jewish man called Scher. I loved this job as it required taste and imagination. We made pens, from the cellular tubes to the gold inlays – everything except the nibs. It was a small factory with only three employees and I learned quickly and won recognition for my designs. It was fairly well paid and I became one of the family's chief breadwinners.

For making fountain-pens I earned three pengo a week, which was a lot of money if you were in dire straits. For instance, with no kitchen to prepare meals we had to send out for food. For one pengo we could get an entire family meal from the local kosher restaurant. Nothing extravagant, but enough to feed the family.

Munky also worked long hours. From early in the morning he laboured in a large knitwear factory on the outskirts of Budapest, standing all day by the dusty machines. In the evenings, when he was not at the yeshivah, he gave private tutorials in English and French. Max also managed to make money by teaching English. This way we managed to save some money and eventually we rented a larger flat. We moved another two times before eventually settling down near the Danube where Max, Munky and I shared a bedroom.

It was during this time that I fell ill. The years of sporadic eating and tension had begun to have their effect on me. My nervousness increased as I was further subjected to anti-Semitic abuse in Budapest, especially when Mr Scher sent me to collect the money that people owed for the pens. My Hungarian was very poor, which made any business dealings problematic and often customers refused to pay up, hurling racist comments at me. Returning to my boss without the money meant receiving more abuse from him.

What made matters even worse was that one of the employees in the fountain-pen workshop, Ilyés Lajos, was a Hungarian fascist. He regularly made anti-Semitic remarks, despite the fact that his boss was Jewish. I began to get serious stomach pains and often could not continue my work due to the agony. Mr Scher's wife noticed this and, because she had always liked me, took me to her doctor who diagnosed stomach ulcers.

Strangely enough, Ilyés grew to like me as time went on and gave me all kinds of little tasks. Because he was my superior I had to go and fetch his lunch for him every day, which meant running to the other end of town where his mother lived in a street behind the main railway station. As soon as Ilyés explained where she lived, I realised I was going to traverse yet another red-light district. The first time I hurried to Ilyés's mother, I was surrounded by young women trying to entice me from my errand. By the third or fourth day, I had become a regular and they often waved at me as I hurried by.

Ilyés's mother made the most beautiful sandwiches. As soon as I had left her home for the first time, I took a peek in the box. At that time our family was struggling and we had to make do with very little. But I was so scared of Ilyés that I did not dare help myself to some of his lunch.

So every day I ran to his mother, through the crowd of working girls, and on Monday mornings Ilyés's favourite habit was to brag about his sexual exploits over the weekend, trying to make me blush – which he succeeded in doing. When he told me stories about the different women he had trifled with, I thought of Medy and wondered if I would ever see her again.

My wishes were fulfilled somewhat one Saturday morning in the spring of 1942. I was coming out of the Dohany synagogue with Munky and my father; a warm day and people were standing and chatting in the square. Adjusting my eyes to the light as I stepped into the sunshine, I noticed a group of girls standing a short distance away. My heart stopped when I saw Medy among them. She was wearing a hat, had grown taller and was looking even more beautiful than before. She glanced in my direction and, as our eyes met, her body jolted in recognition.

Father assumed that I was just gawking at a group of girls and angrily pushed me away and round the corner before I had a chance to explain. Munky, as ever, commented on how improper my behaviour was. As Father pulled me along, I made an excuse about having left something in the synagogue and ran back to the square. But when I got there, the girls had already left. The square was now quiet. Desperately I ran in all directions but Medy was gone. I had longed to see her again and now that I had, I had lost her just as abruptly as before. I went regularly to Dohany synagogue with my father, but she did not return there.

Despite everything, love was in the air – for the girls at least. Else married Bernat, a blow for Hedwig who had lost her fiancé but had to wear a smile on her face for her younger sister. Lillie met André, a man of precarious fortunes who dealt in import and export. 'If you marry that man, you'll regret it,' Father warned Lillie. But she turned down his advice in favour of a dashing husband. And lived to rue that fateful choice.

Hedwig was saved when she met a kindly looking man with a limp in a public swimming-pool. His name was Tibor and it was love at first sight.

So with three daughters married or engaged, my father thought that life would carry on as before and continued to insist that Munky and I went to the local yeshivah in the evenings – the Tiferet Bachurim – where we read the Torah and the Talmud in Hebrew. We studied for three hours each evening. Sometimes, if there was enough money, we went to a concert or an opera – but that was a real treat. Most of the time we went to the yeshivah. Father also tried to get me into a choir – partly to continue my training and partly because choristers received a little payment for their time. Unfortunately, my voice was close to breaking and no choirmaster would take me. 'Let his voice have a good rest. If you don't, it will be damaged for life and he will never become a cantor,' he was warned.

Occasionally, when Munky and I were rushed for time, we would go to a Mizrachi shul to pray because it was so close to our flat. This time Father did not protest, but he still refused to talk reasonably about the future; Palestine was still a taboo subject. Munky, however, was beginning to show an increasing interest in Zionism. I saw less and less of him, especially after he made friends with a young man called Gyuri Morgenstern.

In the autumn of 1943, Father had started to frequent a different shul. On Saturdays he would grab his coat and his sons and take us to the Polisher shul, where an extraordinary rabbi preached – my brother, Max, had originally heard him when he had attended a friend's wedding in the village of Munkacs in the late 1930s. He was an extremely orthodox but gifted orator. In the early 1940s he had moved to Budapest and his reputation spread. He spoke in the most beautiful Yiddish and people clamoured to get to his lectures.

At that time the situation for the Jewish people in Budapest was worsening by the day. There was no German occupation, but the government sympathised and collaborated with the Nazis. Anti-Semitism was rife both in the Hungarian army and the police force. From 1941 many men were taken to forced-labour camps, where those actually were no one knew, as the majority were never heard of again. Before leaving, many of these men came to the rabbi and, kissing his hands, begged for a blessing. I used to see them in the mornings as I popped into the Polisher shul to say my prayers on my way to work.

But, no matter how desperate the situation became, most people still believed that all the suffering was part of a divine master plan that would come to fruition any day now with the coming of the Messiah. They indulged themselves in religious devotion. On Saturday afternoons the rabbi's followers would gather round his table for the third, compulsory meal of the Shabbat. To get Shirajim, some of the leftovers from the rabbi's table, was one of the great merits. Ordinary mortals, like my father, were confined to the regular pews.

On one of these Saturday afternoons, late in 1943, father, Munky and myself were sitting there as usual when we noticed the rabbi begin to rock backwards and forwards in a slow rhythm without uttering a single word. He seemed to be in a trance-like state. Was he communing with God? Whatever he was doing, it seemed to go on for an eternity.

Hours passed; outside the street lights were lit. The congregation was perplexed, it was by now long past the conclusion of the Shabbat.

Suddenly the rabbi threw up his arms vehemently towards heaven, as if he were physically trying to get hold of God. He stayed in that position for quite some time and then burst out into the most frightening roar, pleading: 'God, what are you waiting for? If you don't help now it will soon be too late.'

Then, screaming even louder with a weeping cry, he challenged God: 'Make us believe in you. Don't let us down. Show yourself now. Don't wait, don't wait, please don't wait any longer.'

Complete silence followed. I could hear my father weeping quietly. I did not know what to think. If the rabbi was questioning God's silence and inaction, then who could we go to for spiritual reassurance? Perhaps God no longer cared what happened to his people? Perhaps he had no control over the Nazis? Perhaps the Messiah was no longer coming?

We were all shaken, overcome with emotion at the rabbi accusing the Divine, not capable of looking at each other in the eye. God's silence was as unbearable as it was bleak. Then a Chassid, who had been sitting near the rabbi, broke into the tune of grace after the meal. He sang powerfully, trying to fill the vacuum with religious fervour and hope. He himself was desperately close to tears and we all joined in the grace, all of us not wanting to face reality; that our fate was sealed.

That evening as we walked home, father held our hands, reciting prayers of forgiveness for the rabbi who had dared to put God on trial. God's silence was not to be questioned, only the rabbi's loss of faith. The rabbi's outcry had not awoken any of the congregation, or indeed my father, to the ominous reality that was encroaching on us. The Nazis had surrounded us; we were not welcome in Budapest; there was no place to go. The Messiah could not save us.

~ • ~

In March 1944 the Germans invaded Hungary.

Munky and I had had to go twice a week for so-called military training in a youth section of the Hungarian army called the Levente. It was compulsory and if you played truant you had to serve two days in prison. Initially, the Levente had been for all boys, whatever their religious or racial origin. However, by the time we had to go, the Jews had been segregated and there was a special division reserved for us. As it was run by pro-Nazi Hungarians, the squad leaders were anti-Semitic and subjected us to punishing exercises as well as verbal and even physical abuse. The whole scheme was designed to be a horrendous experience for Jews.

For a start, one of the compulsory days of attendance was a Saturday which meant breaking Sabbath regulations against working on the sacred day. In addition, the barracks were quite a distance outside town and because we were also forbidden to travel on the Sabbath, the day started off with a gruelling hike so that we were already exhausted before the day's exercises had even begun.

The sergeant who was in charge of our squad was a cruel disciplinarian – the exercises he made us undergo were Olympian. He lashed out at the slightest provocation and the last time we attended training he kicked Munky so hard for a minor transgression that he coughed up blood.

Partly because of that incident and partly because Mr Scher did not like letting me away from work in the middle of the week, Munky and I decided that we were not going to go again. 'Don't worry, nothing will happen to you,' said my boss. 'Just idle threats. You're better staying at work here.'

He was wrong. We were found out and I was summoned to court. Munky, who had not skipped off as frequently as I, got away with a stern warning. At first, I avoided going to court but when I finally did go to hear my sentencing, I received four, rather than the customary two, days' sentence.

A family council was called to decide what should be done.

'Four whole days in Mozsar prison. Anything could happen to him in there,' worried my mother.

'No, they just get you to do some community service, you know, cleaning up, that sort of thing. That's what I've heard anyway,' chipped in Karl. 'What do you think?' he asked my father.

Father simply shrugged his shoulders. He certainly did not want me to go but did not have any alternatives to suggest.

'What if Ernest doesn't go at all?' asked Munky.

'No,' said Fritz firmly. 'Now, with the Germans looking over their shoulders, the authorities are acting on the slightest provocation.' He was right. 'It would be best if Ernest just went and did his time in there. If he doesn't show up it could just blow up in our faces.'

So the matter was decided. I was to go. Little did we know what was to follow.

3

THE ROAD TO AUSCHWITZ

~

On the morning of Thursday, 13 April 1944, I was sent off to undergo my punishment for skipping Levente service. Mother had packed me a rucksack full of kosher food with a clean change of underwear. She had packed and repacked the bag as if she was trying to deny to herself that her boy was going to prison.

'Come on, Therezia, that's enough,' said my father, taking hold of the rucksack.

'I'm not sure I've packed everything though.'

'Yes, you have.' And Father took me by the hand out of the door. Mother did not turn around as I left the flat.

We had to go to Mozsar police station and, as we walked into the building, my father handed over my summons to the policeman behind the counter at the end of the long entrance hall.

'Right, Mr Löwy,' said the man glancing at the piece of paper, 'you can leave your son here.' He was very matter-of-fact and did not even look at me.

Father hesitated. I had just turned nineteen but in his eyes I was still his little son. He was more nervous than I was.

'He'll be all right. You just go home now, Mr Löwy.'

But father was reluctant to leave.

'Don't worry. He'll be safe as houses in here.'

Somewhat reassured, my father let go of my hand. 'Right, then. I'll be back in four days. You behave yourself now,' he instructed me, trying to act like the stern father of a delinquent. He began to walk out of the station and then he stopped and turned round to have another look at me. He smiled and tried to look brave and encouraging, then he disappeared out of the door. It was the last I ever saw of him.

What neither my father nor any of my family knew was that if your sentence was above two days, you were taken to the proper prison at Mosonyi on the outskirts of the city. For me, Mosonyi was only the beginning of a sentence that would last until 1945.

~ • ~

The police station on Mozsar Street had a large room where all the prisoners were locked up together. There were two wooden benches on either side, and, as it was still early in the morning, I was alone and sat down on one of the benches. Suddenly I heard the key turn in the lock and a young woman was shoved into the room. The officer with her pushed her onto the wooden bench opposite me and pointing his finger menacingly at her and said, 'Stay put. You don't cross over the room and talk to that young boy. Got it? Or else there'll be trouble.'

No sooner had the officer slammed the heavy door behind him than the young lady was at my side. She looked like the sort of woman Ilyés enjoyed spending his money on. My heart was pounding as she edged closer and closer to me. She was tall and stunningly beautiful; her tousled, golden hair was splayed across the red fox fur collar of her camel-hair coat. Underneath she was wearing a red velvet dress with white buttons up the front. The lower buttons were undone and she was exposing the most beautiful legs I had ever seen. In fact, they were the only woman's legs that I had ever seen outside the family home.

'Perhaps you'd like to sit over there,' I suggested softly. 'I don't want to see you getting into trouble.'

But she began to play with my hair, twisting it around her fingers, and said, 'Don't be like that. You're such an innocent, aren't you? So young.'

She then looked me deep in my eyes and said, 'My name is Klari. I'm young too. I'll be twenty next week.'

Looking closer she clasped her hands and suddenly announced, 'You're Jewish, aren't you? I don't agree with all this rubbish they're saying on the streets about you. It's awful the way some people behave.'

In a low voice she continued, 'I love Jewish men. You're much more . . . appreciative . . .' trying to find the right word, '. . . considerate.' Immediately she kissed me.

I was stunned, but even more so when I heard the key turn in the lock once more. I tried to escape her embraces but the officer saw us and cursing this blonde-haired woman, he man-handled her back to the other side of the room.

At the same time a middle-aged man with a bloody nose and swollen eyes was pushed through the door. He landed heavily on the floor and remained there. Shuffling himself into a more comfortable position, he eventually fell asleep. His elephantine snoring soon echoed around the cell.

When the police had left and this new man was fully asleep, Klari returned to my side and whispered, 'Want to know why I'm here? They said I stole some man's wallet – fifty pengos they said was inside it.'

She deliberately opened her eyes wide, trying to look as innocent as possible. Then as quick as a flash she produced a bundle of notes and rammed them down my socks, explaining, 'They'll search me. But they won't search you.'

The other prisoner did not stay asleep long and soon he was banging on the door to be allowed to go to the toilet. But, as the door opened, the policemen had another destination in mind and we were ordered into a van, the Black Maria, and were taken to Mosonyi prison. I was confused at this change in plan but did not argue. Klari smiled to reassure me. The van was windowless and was already full of prostitutes and other criminals who had been picked up that night.

'Keep well clear of that boy,' the officer again warned Klari as he shut the van door behind us. But within seconds of the van leaving the station she was again at my side, wriggling herself onto my lap and putting her arms around me. From the driver's cab one of the officers spotted us and ordered the driver to stop. Throwing open the back doors the officer leapt into the van in a fury. Unfortunately, he had misjudged the height of the van ceiling and very nearly knocked himself unconscious in mid-air. But Klari jumped out of the van and kissed his head better whilst mopping up the blood with her handkerchief. She talked to him like a mother fussing over a child who had fallen off a swing. Despite her wildness she was obviously still innocent in many ways – and caring.

Klari was hauled back into the van and we set off again for Mosonyi prison. When we arrived the men were separated from the women; Klari's parting words were: 'Listen to me, as soon as you get out of here, your first journey will be to Madame Clarisse on Kiraly Street. That's where I work. You won't regret it. I guarantee.'

We were marched to the 'Mousehole' or, in Hungarian, *Egeres*, which was the nickname given to the common cell. Within minutes my rucksack was raided and I was left with nothing. During the day more and more people were pushed into the cell, including one aggressive-looking young man who was still in handcuffs. As night fell I lay down on my empty rucksack watching the different characters of the Budapest underworld. I pulled myself deeper and deeper into my corner and hoped that no one would notice me.

About midnight I heard a noise in the corridor. Looking out through a crack in the door, I saw a very finely dressed Jewish gentleman and a beautiful, well-dressed girl in the company of two guards. The couple were separated, much to the woman's distress, and the door of the Mousehole opened. The finely dressed gentleman landed on the floor of our shared cell in an indecorous manner. He looked round forlornly.

The next morning, before anyone woke up, I put on my philacteries [two boxes placed on the heart and the head] and moved into a clear space to say my morning prayers. As I stepped over the slumbering bodies, the man suddenly looked at me and whispered, 'Pray for me as well.'

Just then the door opened and a tall, middle-aged officer entered.

'Ledermann!'

The man looked up, confused. The officer repeated the name and the dazed man got up and left the cell.

A short while later the same police officer returned and called out my name. I answered and he took me outside. We marched along the corridor and he explained that I was being taken to do communal work. Suddenly he stopped and, turning round, examined me closely.

'You want to eat kosher?'

Without thinking about the consequences of admitting to being Jewish I answered, 'Yes, of course.' I was concerned only with the fact that I was famished, as I had not eaten anything in twenty-four hours. The guard led me into a great hall where Jewish families were sitting, and as the door behind me closed, I heard the key turning in the lock.

I immediately went over to get some breakfast when I saw Ledermann, now with the girl again. He spotted me.

'Don't tell me,' Ledermann smiled. 'He asked you whether you wanted to eat kosher?'

I nodded and Ledermann laughed and invited me to sit with him. He told me that the girl was his daughter and his family earned their money through owning a chain of exclusive cinemas in Bratislava. They had no idea why they were there, or why all these other Jewish families were crowded into the same room. We had all heard rumours and now that the Germans had invaded Hungary, who could tell what was going to happen next? Everyone's greatest fear was the labour camp. I began to realise that my fate was somehow entangled with the Ledermanns and that communal work was the last thing the authorities had planned for me.

At midday we were taken outside into the yard and lined up and, as we were marched out of the yard, I was separated from Ledermann and his daughter. The guards looked at us impassively and through the crowd I saw Klari staring at us and crying; she was sobbing her heart out. Perhaps she had been told our destination, I do not know, but the sight of us seemed to cause her distress.

Hungarian mounted police drove us through the streets of

the capital. They shouted at us and lashed out with their whips, trying to impress the Germans who followed in their motor-cars. I twisted and turned, trying to see a friendly face – maybe someone who knew me could get word to my family – but I saw no more friendly faces. As Kraijchirovich had done in Brat-islava, the people thronging the streets of Budapest to get a good view of our humiliation, smiled as we were taken away. The only human showing us any pity was the young Hungarian prostitute.

We were marched to a nearby railway station. As we moved closer I could make out the figures of Germans in SS uniforms. I began to panic but there was no one to ask where we were going to be taken. The SS herded us onto cattle trucks; there were about eighty people crammed into each car. It all went very smoothly and no one seemed to protest. I tried to see where the Ledermanns had got to, but the doors were suddenly banged shut and then I heard them being sealed from the outside. They did not open again until thirty hours later.

The deportation of Hungarian Jewry had started and, without realising it, I was to be part of the first load from Budapest. We were locked up in the wagon with no access to food, water or toilets, with the only air and light coming from a tiny window above our heads which had barbed wire stretched across the opening. In one way we were lucky, we travelled in April when the temperature was mild.

I glanced around me. We all looked as disbelieving as each other. Some started to pray, others were moaning softly, a few were arguing. As the hours passed the air became stale. People struggled to snatch at the tiniest of spaces in order to stretch their legs or backs. More voices were raised and fighting broke out. There was no space to get into a comfortable position. No water to satisfy our raging thirst. Crying children refused to be pacified. Their high-pitched whining grated on our nerves. Even rich and cultured people fought a losing battle against their basic instincts and joined in the squabbling. Until a few hours ago they had been enjoying the pleasures of their beautiful homes, now they found themselves and their children in inhuman conditions and they were unable to do a thing about it.

The critical factor was the lack of a toilet, and as the hours passed, we became the victims of our own bodies. The other torment was the insecurity of not knowing for how long we would be away for, how long we would be locked up for, or where our final destination was. I knew nobody in our compartment. The arguments turned into out-and-out warfare. It was a horrifying journey.

After some thirty hours or so, the train slowed down and through a gap in the door I could see a Polish name printed in big letters on a platform sign. None of us had ever heard of the name before. The train suddenly jolted to a stop and then we started going backwards. We shunted along a new length of track for about half an hour. Through the gaps we could make out the terrain: it was the very desolate, grey, flat countryside of Auschwitz.

The train stopped and, managing to squirm my way to the window, I could see more clearly. Outside in the distance there were thousands of little red flowers fluttering about. Later I found out that those red flowers were in fact women, all wearing red headscarves. Then I saw men in SS uniforms running up to the platform with savage dogs that strained at their chains and barked like wild hounds.

From the moment the doors slid back you sensed an inescapable doom and the screaming soldiers and snarling dogs created an atmosphere of panic and chaos. 'Raus! Schnell!' a barrage of orders. We were ordered to leave the cattle trucks. Some who did not leave fast enough, usually children and the elderly who were less agile, were hurled out of the trucks. The next sensation you became aware of was an unbearable but unidentifiable stench.

A group of elegantly dressed officers arrived by open-top Mercedes and walked casually onto the ramp. Later I found out that a particularly striking-looking one among them had been Joseph Mengele. They began the 'selection' – left, right. It was all so routine for the SS. They did not really look at you and even found time to crack jokes among themselves. With a simple nod of the head, the light flick of the hand or a riding crop, families were separated; husbands from wives, brothers from sisters, parents from children – except mothers with young children and babies. We did not know then why they were kept together, it was only later that we discovered that it was in order to ensure that the children did not panic as they entered the gas chambers. People were pleading to stay together, but no matter how much they begged it made absolutely no difference. Ironically, healthy adults did not know that only by being separated from their young children or their elderly parents could they have a chance of surviving.

Suddenly, in the tumult, Ledermann appeared. He ran in and out of my column like a tornado, screaming up and down the line like he had lost his mind.

'Eva!'

He did not see me. A couple of guards tried to catch him, but he had the energy of a madman. Suddenly he threw himself on the ground, thrashing the earth with his fists, sobbing for his daughter; 'Eva, Eva, I want my daughter!'

But his beautiful daughter was nowhere in sight. They may have been separated from each other at the station in Budapest or just some moments ago. The guards dragged him off the ground. He was clinging to the earth with his nails like an animal. 'Eva!' he sobbed once again.

Nobody was interested in the old man's cries; he was just one of the countless tragedies, one of a legion hysterical with grief. I never saw him again.

I ended up in a group of about five hundred men. We had been selected to live – although I still did not realise that at the time. By the time we were marched into the camp at about six o'clock that evening, there was a group of several thousand people waiting there already who had arrived on other trains. If we still did not understand the new world order in this place then it was vividly brought home to us by the actions of a Jewish kapo as we stood waiting in the cold evening breeze. A man who had arrived with us simply went up to the kapo to ask what seemed like a fairly innocuous question. The kapo's face contorted, he grabbed hold of the prisoner and beat him to death with a truncheon. I had never seen anyone being killed before. It was the beginning of my induction to camp life.

We were taken away to a blockhouse and told to undress. All our clothes were taken from us as were our belongings. Naked, we waited there for hours, not knowing what was going to happen next. Abruptly, we were marched into a big hall where each of us had to jump up onto a little platform. Other prisoners hurriedly shaved every hair from our bodies; their razors were blunt and scraped our skin. No dignity. No mercy. I came away bleeding from every part of my body. Then we were herded through an archway where men waited with a sponge and a bucket of disinfectant. They roughly doused the stinging solution all over our bodies; it went into our eyes, our recently acquired cuts, the grazes and in our back passage.

From there we were herded into a shower room. We were packed tightly together. Minutes passed. Then, suddenly, the taps were opened and we were assaulted by boiling hot water from every side. There was no space to move away as the water burned our mutilated skin. People were jumping around like mad monkeys, screaming in pain. I was shaking terribly. A mad scene. I did not know whether to laugh or cry. My body decided for me and suddenly my screaming turned into laughter. The combination of the sheer pain, shock and the experience of the last two days produced in me an uncontrollable laughing fit. Briefly I went totally insane.

By the end of that Saturday we were totally exhausted. Wearing striped pyjamas, ludicrously too big or too small, and still having had no food or water, we were sent to block eleven in Birkenau. There were no toilet facilities in block eleven and I was desperate to relieve myself – I had last been that night in Mosonyi prison and it was now over forty-eight hours since then. Yet I simply could not do it. In block eleven the urine was ankle deep as people relieved themselves wherever they were standing or, if they were too weak, where they were lying. The stench was unbearable; the odour of urine, dirt and sweat mingled with that strange smell I had noticed upon my arrival.

Completely exhausted, I fell onto a bunk where three or four men were lying. I must have fallen asleep, as the next thing I remember is hysterical laughter. I opened my eyes to see faces pressed into the grille above me. They belonged to Polish-Jewish prisoners who had been in Auschwitz for a while. They had sneaked over to our block to warn us about the camp. Laughing, they shouted in Yiddish.

'Don't worry. You will not stay here long. You'll escape up the chimney.'

And they gestured to some tall chimneys, which we had seen in the distance, with smoke billowing out of them. It was then that I realised what that other smell was. Some of the older men around me began to pray and call on God. But the Poles just laughed and screamed, 'Prayers will not help you. Don't put your trust in God. There's no escaping the chimneys.'

That was the first night in Auschwitz. Just two days before we had lived a relatively normal life with a name and an identity. Now we had a little number on a metal plate. We were no longer human beings but objects. No hair, no name, no dignity, no hope. People could do whatever they liked with you. We were at the mercy of madmen.

~ • ~

The smell was the worst thing about Auschwitz, especially after the revelations of that night when we realised what our nostrils were inhaling; burnt human flesh. It lay on your chest and tore your lungs apart, making it impossible to breathe. People apparently managed to survive in Auschwitz for years; I do not know how they did it.

The following day I was still unable to relieve myself and the pain was excruciating as we had to stand up straight to pose for photographs for the SS. We did nothing for several days – except listen to what the others said about the guards, the selections, the kapos, the gas chambers and crematoria. My world was turned upside down, back to front and inside out. I thought of father returning to the police station on Monday morning and not knowing where his son was.

After nearly a week in Auschwitz a rumour went out that there was going to be a selection in our barracks and the adjacent ones. We had learned by now that the word 'selection' was synonymous with the gas chambers. Perhaps they were weeding out the older and sicker ones. I was still doubled up in pain from not being able to go to the toilet, but I straightened myself up as best as possible. Nevertheless, when the SS came round, I was picked out.

However, I was not designated for death. Instead, about five hundred of us were singled out to leave Auschwitz. I could not believe my ears. Forced labour commandos were needed in another camp and I was considered healthy enough to be put to work. Once again we were herded onto cattle trucks, but I did not care. When the train left the camp I was jubilant, ecstatic, like someone who had lost his senses. I could not stop kissing the walls of that dirty truck for taking me away from that place.

Now I was en route to Wüsegiersdorf, a small labour camp in Upper Silesia.

4

ANTON'S PIPES

~

'Just be a Mensch,' my father had told me. 'Be a human being. Don't be fooled by what anyone else is doing. Just be a Mensch.' My father's homily that we should aspire to live as moral beings acquired a particular resonance in the camps where guards, as well as prisoners, were unable to maintain their humanity and became indifferent to human suffering and turned into beasts.

What makes a man retain his humanity? Because I was there, people scrutinise me for the answer to that question. However, the key to this particular problem still remains elusive. For all I know is what I have experienced: hunger, cold, exhaustion, violence, illness and death. These were the things that determined whether we were vessels for good or evil.

Should you cause pain to another in order to survive? Is lying more acceptable than stealing? Stealing more tolerable than murder? For most of the desperate in the camps the struggle for survival involved no decision at all. For others, the crux of existence was the fight to remain human. They battled to suppress the darker side – the part of you that insidiously whispered: 'Survive at any cost.'

Now, thinking of my father's words, it becomes clear that the tenacity with which we either hold on to our humanity or sink into the mire is conditioned by a lifetime of experience and influences: parents, friends, the system in which we are raised. Most importantly, the influence of those people whose company we happen to be in when we are faced with crucial choices to be made in a split second can determine which path we follow. More often than not, we are not the real masters of our own decisions.

Sometimes choice is completely removed from our realm by those who make decisions about us or for us, like Helmut Palmer, my childhood friend from Bratislava.

Now I can understand him: it was easy to get carried away by the theatre, the marching and the slogans of the régime. I was carried away myself years later by Stalin's slogans. Ideologies which warrant atrocities such as Hitler's racial programme or Stalin's terror came from the age-old antagonisms. These were further aggravated and manipulated. People were easily drawn into the ideological vortex.

In the Wüsegiersdorf camps some men and women refused to be swept along in the tide – guards as well as prisoners. They did not resist openly, but even in these extreme circumstances their humanity came through. They found a simple and, in effect, courageous way to maintain their human integrity.

There I found these people. There was Messinger – the Lagerälteste, appointed by the Germans to represent the prisoners. And others like him: my cousin Leopold, his friend Zoltan, and Walter, a boxer from Vienna. Last but not least, the German workshop supervisor, 'Little Anton' as we called him.

The continued humanity of all these people enabled me to survive both physically and spiritually.

Wüsegiersdorf was a small village in Silesia about sixty miles away from Auschwitz. Nearby was a labour camp which was, by comparison, relatively civilised. The camp resembled a small industrial estate. It was centred around a three-storey brick building, a former textile factory which had been transformed into the prisoners' barracks. By the time we arrived, Polish prisoners had been occupying the ground floor for some time. As it was the Polish who were first incarcerated, they were the first to become dehumanised. The majority displayed no feelings for human suffering and the bulk of our kapos in Wüsegiersdorf were Polish.

My group was housed on the third floor of the brick building, while the second floor was shared by a mixture of Germans, Austrians and a few Ukrainians, but the camp consisted mainly of Poles and Hungarians. The central complex was surrounded by a barbed-wire fence. Further away were smaller brick buildings which housed the guards' and officers' quarters.

As Wüsegiersdorf was a labour camp, we received a minimum of food, enough to keep you on your feet but no more. There was not really a sufficient amount for young men engaged in hard manual labour. Sometimes someone's generous actions showed that humanity and goodness had survived in some of us – among us was an old Polish man with his teenage son and I saw a couple of times how he gave his portion to the boy. As eating meant surviving and lack of food meant certain death, this was an incredibly selfless deed.

~ • ~

~

Work began at five in the morning with the roll-call on the Appelplatz which was situated in the courtyard of the former textile factory. Then the Kommandos [work units] would line up by the camp's big wooden gate to be dispatched.

Naturally, the local inhabitants of the village knew about the camp. During the first few months I was on a building commando and we worked outside the complex. Walking through the village, and the neighbouring village of Oberwüsegiersdorf and Charlottenbrün, from where we would fetch sand and stones, the clattering of our wooden shoes on the cobbled streets would draw attention to our presence.

Wüsegiersdorf was run by a mixture of SS men, soldiers and civilians. This meant there was an enormous difference in attitude between the various guards. The SS had undergone a particularly sadistic and ideologically based training, but among soldiers and civilians you occasionally found more normal people.

Our survival depended on how you weighed up the individual guards – who it was safe to talk to and who was considered an unpredictable savage. It was often a question of eye contact. I would risk looking a guard straight in the face searching for a flicker of humanity behind the eyes. Once eye contact had been made, you were recognised as a human being, not a numbered Untermensch. Whenever that relationship was established, however tenuous it might appear, you had at least a glimmer of hope: the odd scrap of food, a little protection.

The German in charge of our section was called Schwartz. He kept absolute discipline through being a Jekyll and Hyde character – sometimes fair, other times completely unpredictable in his behaviour.

His savage side came to the fore when Messinger, the Lager-älteste, was put in charge of the early-morning flogging, which usually took place before the commandos left the camp. We were lined up to witness any punishment that was being meted out. Messinger had been a well-known football player in Bratislava. He was an enormous, virile man about thirty-five years of age, but already completely bald. His prestige was very important for the Germans as it allowed him to keep the other prisoners under control.

On this particular morning one of the guards forced the prisoner to bend over the bench and Messinger was to do the whipping. We knew by now that the number of lashes could be anything from between five and twenty-five, depending on which rule had been breached. Normally, few people survived twenty-five lashes.

Messinger took up the whip and began. Schwartz immediately noticed that Messinger was feigning the power of his strokes. He stormed up to him and shouted; 'If you don't do it properly, I'll do it for you.'

It was a terrible situation for Messinger. His usual answer to the system was one of secret passive resistance. He took up the whip once again and did as he was ordered, his strokes raining down. Even so, we noticed that he was still not really lashing at full power.

~ • ~

It was a Sunday afternoon when we returned from work and saw that the most severe way of punishing prisoners had been prepared – on the Appelplatz, gallows had been erected. Standing nearby was Schwartz's superior, an SS Oberstürmbannführer, who was a much younger man but renowned for being infinitely more sadistic.

Sensing the worst, we stood waiting in the last of the day's sunlight, lined up in front of the gallows platform, not knowing who was to be the object of the Obersturmbannführer's wrath. From the open windows of the officers' quarters, a gramophone recording of Beethoven's Fifth Symphony sliced through the early evening air. Several moments passed, then a door from one of the nearby buildings opened. From the shadows emerged a young, slender boy accompanied by Messinger and an older prisoner. Everybody strained their eyes to see who the boy was.

'That was the youngster caught trying to escape,' the whisper went round the ranks.

Escape – the Obersturmbannführer would show no mercy to those who attempted it. Not even the boy's youth would compel him to show clemency.

'What about the older one?'

'That's his father,' came the reply in a low tone. It was the old Polish man who shared his food with his son.

Not another word was said while the guards instructed the boy to stand on a wooden stool. A coarse rope was placed around his neck. The father could only stare at the ground. The Obersturmbannführer went up to the father and said: 'Not like that. Look up. Up there at the gallows.'

The man slowly raised his head and stared his son in the face.

'That's better,' the Obersturmbannführer continued. 'Because, you see, I want you to look at your child while he dies.'

The SS officer made a gesture to Messinger and all eyes turned to the Lagerälteste.

'Proceed,' he ordered sharply, pointing at the stool under the boy's feet and meaning that Messinger should kick it away.

Messinger, however, remained motionless. The Obersturmbannführer was dumbfounded.

'Did you hear me?'

Messinger again made no acknowledgement. The Obersturmbannführer became livid and, marching up to him, he shouted in the Lagerälteste's face: 'You have one minute or every tenth prisoner will be shot dead,' adding, somewhat significantly: 'It's your decision.'

Still Messinger did not budge and the Obersturmbannführer became apoplectic, striding up and down our column. He screamed a last warning at all of us: 'Within two minutes every fifth prisoner will be shot until somebody volunteers to kick the stool away.'

The poor boy was still standing there with the rope around his neck, his father positioned only a couple of yards away. Neither Messinger nor anybody else made a move.

Suddenly a small Polish kapo, normally a quiet man, ran from his group and kicked the stool away. There was a short-lived moment of strange, selfish relief. Then it dawned on us that the rope was too long. It took an age for the boy to die, half-hanging there, his toes brushing against the ground. All the time we had to stand there, watching his face contort until we heard the last breath rasping out from his mouth.

During those months in Wüsegiersdorf Messinger continued to resist the dehumanisation process. He maintained his astuteness and sense of fair play even under duress, as my friend Walter was to find out.

~ • ~

Before the war, Walter had been an amateur boxer. A strong, stocky and stout man in his early twenties, he came originally from Vienna but had started a philatelist shop in Budapest. For some unknown reason he had been allocated a bunk bed on the ground floor of the barracks building. There he suffered endlessly at the hands of the Polish kapos who constantly tried to humiliate him because of his reputation as a strong man.

Walter and I were inseparable. He often helped me in difficult situations, risking his own life for me. But one Sunday he came up to the third floor. He scooped up my belongings and blanket and said: 'Ernesty, you come and sleep on my floor, in my bunk.' He always called me Ernesty. There was no arguing with him and he dragged me downstairs.

The Poles were not yet back from work. Walter settled me in. As soon as the other prisoners appeared I realised our mistake as a hundred hostile eyes swooped down on me. One of the Poles skirted Walter and looked threateningly at me.

'What's he doing in our quarters?' the Pole demanded.

'He's my friend. What business is it of yours?'

Walter's defiance only infuriated the Pole further. Before I knew what happened he had belted Walter in the face. That gesture acted as a signal and suddenly Walter found himself under a mound of belligerent Poles.

From nowhere Messinger entered, hauled people away and ordered an end to the fracas. But Walter, now suddenly liberated from under the others, instinctively landed a punch on the first available person's face. Unfortunately, that person was Messinger.

Walter immediately froze, realising what he had done in his blind fury. Likewise, the whole block went quiet, only the resonance of exhausted breathing filled the dense and ominous hush. We all thought that Walter had irrevocably sealed his own fate.

The boxer and the Lagerälteste stared at each other; a furious clash was expected. Instead, Messinger looked at me, saw my belongings on the bunk and simply said: 'Take your things back upstairs.' Then he turned and walked away. In an instant he had gauged the situation and found the solution. That was Messinger: his even temper and unassuming quick thinking saved more than one person from a beating and even death. He never seemed to allow himself to descend into the petty squabbles of survival.

It required a considerable degree of character to live as Messinger did and there were many who could not endure that path. Such a person was Vazsonyi Janos, the son of a pre-war Hungarian Finance Minister. Vazsonyi was an outstanding gentleman in his late thirties. He arrived at Wüsegiersdorf in a pathetic state. Still, he became a great asset to our Sunday evening cultural 'meetings' with his memorable stories. We gradually brought him back to life, but hunger eventually reduced him beyond repair.

We had no toilets in our barracks and we used buckets which were situated on each floor. A rota had been devised: each prisoner was required to take a shift lasting two hours in which it was his responsibility to carry the buckets down the three floors of the building to where they were emptied and cleaned. It was an unpleasant but necessary job. Vazsonyi must have seen the half piece of bread which I had managed to save and he begged to take over my shift in exchange for the food in my hand. I was horrified.

'Please, Vazsonyi, don't ask this of me. Don't do this to yourself. It's not worth it.'

'Ernest, really – you'll be doing me a favour.'

His eyes betrayed hunger and after a moment I said, 'Here, take the bread. The work doesn't matter.'

'It matters,' he replied. And he took the bread saying, 'Now I'll do your turn at the buckets.'

Then, thanking me, he did my shift in exchange for that mouthful of bread. I suspect he also did the same for others. It was difficult to watch a man of such great stature sink so low.

Like Vazsonyi, we were all put to the test. For me it came during one of those moments when choice became, in actuality, a farcical charade. This was to be one of the worst moments of my entire experience in the camp.

Schwartz had gone on leave and a young SS officer from the Eastern Front stepped in. He was a creature who enjoyed inflicting agony on people with a smile engrained on his face. His behaviour simply defied rational motivation. For that reason he belonged to that species of German that was the most dangerous of all.

In the morning before work we were all lined up on the Appelplatz and this young SS officer told us that electricians were needed in Grossrozen.

The mention of Grossrozen struck horror in us. It was a notorious camp, located not far from Wüsegiersdorf, where a free hand was given to brutal kapos. According to the stories we heard, these kapos took daily pleasure in humiliating and killing as many people as possible. In Wüsegiersdorf we had our fair share of flogging and hanging, but Grossrozen meant the ultimate in human cruelty. The Germans used the threat of Grossrozen and punishment often came in the form of transportation to that camp. There was no hope of return.

'Elektriker austreten!' the SS officer sang with a smile on his face.

Now, everybody knew that Walter's secondary occupation was as an electrician.

'Elektriker austreten!' the SS officer continued to sing, walking up and down the line with that grating smile on his face. Walter could only remain rooted, hiding in the crowd, willing himself to disappear.

The SS officer repeated his invitation once more in his sing-song fashion to the recalcitrant electricians on the Appelplatz. Still nobody volunteered. Those few moments of waiting became an eternity.

'Come on, you.' One of the kapos who knew Walter strode up to him and pushed him out of line.

Standing apart from the rest of us he suddenly looked terribly vulnerable. He turned to me and, with an unimaginable desperation in his eyes, he begged: 'Ernesty, come.'

His expression struck my emotions. 'Ernesty, please, come!' But I was unable to move. Panic and shame engulfed me. I tried to tear my eyes from his.

'Ernesty!' his voice rose in urgency, like a small animal being boxed up. I was abandoning him and he knew it.

'Please! Ernesty!'

The SS officer struck Walter across the face with the back of his hand for his insolence. Blood sprang out of Walter's nose. Still he kept pleading with me, 'Ernesty, come on, please!' Tears began to mix with his blood. Yet he continued to implore me to go with him.

Those few moments with him beseeching me to go were the most heartbreaking I had experienced until then. How could I refuse my best friend's begging request. But, in the end, I did not go. The decision only took a few seconds, perhaps less. It saved my life. Walter was taken away and I never saw my friend again.

Did I do the right thing? To have gone would have been an act of suicide and, in the end, I would not have been able to save Walter. But I abandoned a friend – one who had put himself at risk for me.

Was I giving in and becoming indifferent to human suffering? Fortunately, other prisoners helped me to find a way to maintain my humanity. Two such prisoners were my cousin

Leopold and his friend Zoltan. Through them I became acquainted with Anton, a remarkable German gentleman, who was to change the course of my life.

Leopold Pozsonyi – a well-built, handsome young man – was actually my second cousin – his mother and my father were cousins. I had met Leopold when our family was thrown out of Bratislava and we visited Paszto, a little Hungarian peasant village. Leopold had been about sixteen or seventeen at that time. His father had dealt in animal skins. Within this peasant community Leopold's family was considered the *crème de la crème*.

I ran into Leopold again – quite literally – on the first day after arrival in Wüsegiersdorf. It had been a rather strange meeting. A small group of us who had just arrived sat on a hillside in our pyjama uniforms with matching 'Mütze' [caps] while we were waiting to be moved into our block. Somebody suggested saying the afternoon prayer; at the end of the Amidah [the standing silent meditation], I moved back the obligatory three steps and fell over a prisoner who had already finished his prayers and sat down. That is how I found Leopold.

Despite our much changed appearance we recognised each other immediately. It was an emotional moment, we embraced and our eyes filled with tears. Rapidly we exchanged the fragments of news we each had. Neither of us really knew what had happened to our families, but we feared the worst. All we could gather was that our Uncle Hugo, a beloved and wonderful man, had also been transported from Budapest, but he had never left Auschwitz.

Leopold had a Hungarian friend, Zoltan Mérer. These two rough and fearless rowdies had become two of the most envied people in the camp. They managed to wangle themselves into the food store commando and were able to organise special provisions for the inmates which were smuggled into the barracks.

One Friday I returned to our floor to discover that Leopold and Zoltan had managed to filch some barrelled, pickled herring. Fridays being Shabbat, it was customary to eat fish. The appearance of the herring was considered a small miracle. I stared incredulously at the barrel while Leopold and Zoltan handed out the fish.

I said: 'Leopold? How can this be possible?'

'Don't ask,' he laughed and waved me away with his hand.

'But surely this must be dangerous for you. If one of the guards found that food was missing . . .'

'I told you, it's not a problem,' he cut in. 'I've seen to it.'

'How?'

'Well, the guard in charge of the food store is a woman – a German woman.'

He did not elaborate and I stared at him uncomprehendingly. Zoltan, standing listening nearby, was smiling to himself. I could not understand his apparent amusement and, irritated, pressed on.

'So?'

'Well, I've seen to it – that's all. I've arranged it with her to our mutual satisfaction.' Then he added mysteriously, 'It just requires a little give and take – that's all.'

'Well, what did you give her?'

'What did I give her?'

Leopold smirked and drawing me close to him with one of his powerful arms, he breathed: 'What do you think?'

Zoltan and Leopold could not contain themselves as they saw the realisation of what had transpired between the female guard and my cousin slowly materialise on my face.

Being in their position, Zoltan and Leopold had a powerful

status. If Schwartz (who had no control over the food store) needed anything, or if any of the kapos wanted a little something extra, they went to Leopold and Zoltan. And because they were so useful to both the kapos and those officers who had become corrupted, my cousin and his friend had a slightly untouchable aura.

By September 1944 I was still working in the open air on building sites. The frightening prospect of facing the winter armed with only meagre food and inadequate clothing loomed unavoidably. Fortunately, Leopold stepped in. We discussed my fears and within a week I found myself assigned to one of the factory workshops, which was situated just outside the barbed wire with guards encircling the complex every hundred yards or so in little huts. Leopold had gone to Schwartz with two bottles of champagne insisting that I had to be transferred.

The man in charge of the workshop was Anton. He was a smallish, stocky man of about forty. His brown uniform looked tight and uncomfortable, as did the Nazi swastika band on his arm. As a skilled workman he had been drafted into the Organisation Todt – the industrial division of the German war effort. He had about eighty prisoners working for him, mainly repairing military vehicles. This type of work involved toolmaking and precision engineering. However, only less than half of the labourers employed there were skilled in engineering but that, as I discovered, was not a major concern for Anton.

My first day in the workshop started badly. I was as good as lost when I was given a skilled metal job working on an enormous axe with an eight-metre-long lathe. Although I had some experience in engineering, I had never worked on such gigantic and demanding machinery.

Anton, with his hands on his waist, watched me; he soon realised that I was there under false pretences. 'I want to see you in my office in five minutes,' he said as he turned away. Shaking, and with every eye on me, I made my way to his office.

Anton looked up from his desk and watched me for a few seconds. Then he pointed at a fellow prisoner called Sandor Grossman, the Jewish works manager and a highly skilled toolmaker from Transylvania, who was sitting in the corner. 'Look,' Anton said, 'I'm not sending you back. You are to work under this man. He'll teach you how to use the heavy machinery. *Und jetzt 'raus!*'

I could hardly restrain myself from going down on my knees and kissing Anton's feet. There was jubilation in my heart as I left his office. Staying in the factory during the winter months could mean the difference between life and death.

As time went by, Anton kept growing in stature. We never saw him in a bad mood or a rage. There was no one in the factory to supervise him or look over his shoulder, he was in charge and could do what he wanted – provided the SS did not find out. He treated us as human beings: at a time when no German called us by name, he even used our first names. Anton saved us from an almost certain death on the building sites. Many of us had no factory experience but Anton argued that we were indispensable for the work done there.

Even now, fifty years on, his motivation continues to mystify me. Why did he risk himself for us? For the most part he appeared a private and modest man. He had his few favourite workers with whom he would discuss matters and once he even reported to us all how the Red Army was approaching. But apart from that he kept to himself.

You could often see Anton through the glass of his office slowly peeling an apple. With a Swiss army knife and great care he ponderously sliced away the peel so that more often than not it came away in one entire piece, like the spring from the inside of a watch. Then holding the naked apple by the stem, he would devour it, munching through from one end to the other, eating pips and all. The peelings, on a saucer, were presented to one of the prisoners.

It was as if Anton had been unaffected by time. Politics to him were a transient affair, his world was the hierarchy of the workshop. He was a skilled worker and could appreciate those who aspired towards real craftsmanship – earthly achievements to be proud of were the creation of objects of quality craftsmanship. He cared for his workers like a fatherly figure; he took pride in passing on his skills – not invading countries or marching down conquered streets. His values remained unchanged by the Nazi propaganda. In his world the bad things would eventually pass.

That is also why Anton did not give a second thought to assisting a group enterprise which involved smuggling food to other prisoners inside the camp.

~ • ~

The smuggling of food was a hazardous enterprise but ingeniously simple. As part of my job I had to carry large pipes into the camp which were used to repair the stoves in the barracks and the guards' quarters – as an immense amount of wood was burned in the stoves, the pipes would often get choked with soot and debris. The replacement pipes I carried into the camp were about two metres long with a U-bend.

One night, as Leopold was handing out food to a queue of prisoners from his bunk bed which was next to mine, he broached the subject of these pipes.

'One of the stoves downstairs is blocked again,' he commented.

Ernest's grandparents, father and aunt, *c.*1905. Only his grandfather did not perish in the Holocaust; he died in 1942.

ABOVE: Charles in 1929. As the star pupil at rabbinical college, he was chosen to accompany his teacher to Marienbad.

LEFT: Ernest's sister Hedwig and brother-in-law, 1944 – they were both gassed at Auschwitz.

BELOW: Max, Fritz and Hedwig Löwy with a friend in Vienna, 1936.

Alexander Löwy in 1943. In 1944 he was forced to dig his own grave and was then shot in the head by Hungarian Fascists.

Leopold Löwy c.1938. He perished at Buchenwald in 1945.

A mass grave at Belsen. The top left-hand corner was from where Ernest escaped after spending several hours lying amongst the dead and dying.

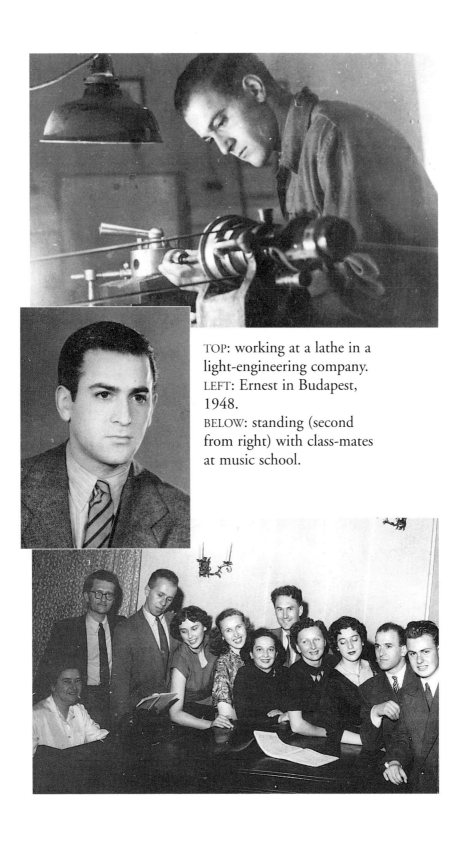

TOP: working at a lathe in a light-engineering company.
LEFT: Ernest in Budapest, 1948.
BELOW: standing (second from right) with class-mates at music school.

TOP LEFT: Fritz in Israel, 1957; TOP CENTRE: Lillie, 1943;
TOP RIGHT: Elsa, 1947.
ABOVE: Charles with his family and mother.

TOP: Ernest in scenes from *The Lost Tribe*, an STV production
which starred Bill Paterson.
ABOVE: With Sir Harry Secombe in *Highway*, 1983.

ABOVE LEFT: Ernest and Kathy's wedding day, 1965; ABOVE RIGHT: Ernest and Kathy in Glasgow, 1966; BELOW: the Reverend Ernest Levy, cantor of Giffnock and Newlands congregation, 1994.

'Is it?' I yawned, pulling the blanket over my head.

'I suppose they'll be sending you to fix it in the next few days.'

'Probably.'

'How often do those things get clogged up, anyhow?'

'There's usually one every week or so to repair.'

Leopold pondered for a moment.

'Do you think anyone would think it strange if two or more stoves got clogged up each week? After all, it's winter.'

I pulled the blanket from off my head and scanned his face.

'What are you driving at, Leopold?'

'How heavy are the pipes? I mean, could you still carry one if something was packed away inside it?'

'Such as?'

'Well, I was thinking that it might be a good way to get larger quantities of food inside the camp. It would also be safer than packing food inside our clothes and risk being sear-ched.'

Leopold had obviously thought this all out before asking me.

'Let me get this straight. You want me to risk my neck smuggling in food rammed down these pipes?'

'Ernest, keep your voice down.' And after a pause, 'Well, what do you think?'

I stared at the rafters picturing the consequences of being discovered.

'Look,' continued Leopold, 'neither myself nor Zoltan could get away with this. The guards would suspect us immediately and this is a whole lot different from smuggling in the odd barrel of herring. If we were caught it could mean . . .'

'Grossrozen,' I concluded for him. There was a moment's silence.

'I wouldn't blame you if you said no. It's just that, well, the guards seem to like you. You're just a boy, a nice boy. It'd never cross their minds that a slip of a lad such as yourself would be involved in such a scheme.'

The dangers involved were racing through my mind.

'I'll let you have time to think about it,' he said and rolled over in his bunk.

'Don't bother, Leopold,' I replied. 'Of course I'll do it.'

For this plan we needed Anton's assistance because he would notice us packing the pipes with food which Leopold or Zoltan delivered to the workshop. It consisted mainly of tinned food – sardines, pilchards and anchovies – usually Belgian. A real windfall was a quantity of dried yellow peas which could be cooked in our workshop and also in the barracks.

Anton not only turned a blind eye, he became actively involved in the smuggling venture. The pipes became known as 'Anton's pipes' because he found a way to stuff both ends of the pipes with rags. This could not be seen and safely sealed the food inside. For a while, I marched at least twice a week into the camp with a ladder in one hand and one of Anton's pipes on my shoulder.

One day I was stopped by Schwartz. 'What are you up to?' I explained there were some repairs to be done in the block. 'How come you speak such good German?' he asked. 'Where are you from?'

'Budapest,' I replied.

'So, you are Hungarian?'

'No, I am not, I am Jewish.'

'Abhauen – disappear,' he said with a barely hidden smile and waved me on.

The smuggling of food became so habitual that I eventually became inured to the possible consequences of my actions.

However, they were brought vividly back to me when I came very close to being discovered.

~ • ~

We were returning to the camp from the workshop one evening and I was loaded with food. Also, I had on two pairs of trousers; the ones on the inside were secured at my ankles with string as inside them were yellow peas. I also had tinned foods tied around my torso, almost as though I was wearing armour. As we approached the gate of the camp, however, a word was whispered from group to group: 'Hippish'. The Hebrew slang meant a warning of trouble, this time we were going to be searched. I was still quite a distance away from the gate but, even so, there was no stepping out of line; I was trapped. I knew that if Schwartz caught me, I would be in Grossrozen in five minutes. A couple of prisoners who had already been caught were sitting on the ground. Five men were waiting at the gate to search us, some of them were kapos, some guards. As I came closer I could see that one of them was Messinger; he was my only hope. I tried to manoeuvre myself into a position so that I would be searched by him and only him.

As I came up to Messinger he put this hands on me, sensed what was going on and hesitated. From a distance, Schwartz immediately noticed something was wrong. 'What's going on over there?' he shouted.

Instantly Messinger struck me across the face and I splayed out across the ground. The Lagerälteste reported to Schwartz that he had found a penknife in my pocket. That was still punishable, but it was not as bad as smuggling food. In that split second of quick-thinking Messinger had saved me once again.

I flew through the gate and walked on. After a while I

realised that one of my trouser legs had loosened and I was trailing a line of yellow peas behind me. Other prisoners came to my aid and kicked the evidence away into the dirt. It was a miraculous escape.

Naturally, this situation could not last forever. One day in the middle of January 1945 the workshop came to a sudden halt. All went quiet when Anton appeared in the company of a much older man who was probably in his sixties and who was also from Organisation Todt. His grey hair was already turning white, he had two metal front teeth, his eyes were close together, which made him a vicious-looking character. Anton announced he had been replaced by this man.

After Anton had spoken quietly and addressed the prisoners with obvious sympathy in his voice, the new man turned to him and said in an ugly, high-pitched voice; 'Because of people like you, we are losing the war.'

To hear a German admitting that they were losing the war was like honey on bread. From behind the machinery I could not resist adding, '*Wir danken dem Führer*' – it was a parody of the customary German response of thanking the Führer instead of God. Unfortunately, like a brazen boy at the back of a classroom, my voice carried further than I had intended.

While everybody held their breath, the new man barked: 'Who was that?' There was nothing to do but to step forward. He put me to one side: 'I'll deal with you later,' and turning to Anton he shouted: 'You're running a holiday camp here! Look, these lazy-bones look far too well fed.' Examining us, he continued, 'I'll bite through your gluttonous gullets, you Hebrew parasites. That will stop you from eating.'

Anton, in his familiar pose with his hands on his hips, asked the new man: 'Maybe you'd like to tell me what crimes these people are supposed to have committed?'

'They brought the war on us, you idiot. Don't you know that?' came the reply.

Anton quipped, 'Obviously you're a lunatic if you honestly believe that,' adding, 'and you can report me for saying that if you like – it makes no difference.'

The new man was furious and in the heat of that confrontation he forgot about me and directed his passion against Anton. In his familiar way Anton had saved me.

That was the last I saw of Anton. I never knew what became of him after that incident. In fact, I never knew anything about the man, about his family or which part of Germany he came from.

One of my lifelong regrets is not being able to thank Anton in person for helping me and so many others. But I will always think of Anton sitting in his office slowly peeling and munching his way through an apple. My family are still amused at how I eat my apples 'Anton-style' in remembrance of him.

~ • ~

After Anton left we got a real taste of the new man's sadism, which earned him the nickname 'the Beast'. Screaming anti-Semitic insults, he prowled around the workshop. For no reason at all, he would lash out at somebody, usually with his boot.

During this time a prisoner called Braun became our new father-figure. Braun had been an accomplished wrestler before the war and we admired his courage, and we had all heard the rumour that during the early days of the camp he had murdered a guard. The story was that in one of the Aussen-kommandos, when groups of prisoners worked in the woods outside the camp, Braun and a particularly unpopular guard had fallen a little behind the marching group. The wrestler had seen his chance and killed the guard. We all wondered why he had not escaped or been found out, but nobody dared to ask him. Naturally, it did no harm to his reputation.

From the beginning there had been a particular animosity between Braun and the Beast, as the wrestler made no secret of his contempt for the German.

One morning Braun was sharpening tools on a grinding wheel while I was nearby breaking up wood for the stove when the Beast appeared and kicked me in the back, roaring: 'You idiot. That wood is too good for burning.'

Braun intervened: 'Leave the boy alone.'

Now the Beast turned his anger on to Braun. He grabbed him, saw that Braun's machine was still working and shoved the poor man's hand in the grinding wheel, but he should not have picked a fight with a wrestler. Braun spun around screaming and there was blood everywhere. He got hold of the Beast and pushed him to the ground, then forced his bleeding hand into the Beast's mouth, shouting: 'Now you can drink Jewish blood. *Schmeckt gut, nicht?*'

Braun was quickly hauled away by other prisoners and the Beast staggered to his feet, lunged out at Braun but lost his balance. He was helped out of the workshop. We never saw the Beast again, Braun disappeared too – the next day he was taken away for 'treatment'.

Less than a month after Anton's dismissal, at the beginning of February 1945, we were assembled. We were told that within ten days the camp was to be evacuated. What that meant exactly, we were unsure of.

If I had thought that had been the ultimate testing ground for our humanity, then I was to be bewildered by what lay ahead: our moral markers were to be driven out to new dimensions that had no clear boundaries. A few mornings later we were lined up to leave the camp, but we had not been informed of our destination.

We were transported to Bergen-Belsen — one of the most notorious concentration camps — which was located many miles away, way up and right across the other end of the country in north-west Germany.

5

THE NIGHT ON THE ELBE

~

About a thousand of us were marched out of Wüsegiersdorf at the beginning of February 1945. The Russian guns could already be heard in the distance. We were split into two groups: one destined for Flossenburg, the other headed for Bergen-Belsen. I was in the second group.

Little did I know what was awaiting us. Throughout the journey to Belsen I was to encounter people who, in their own way, made a stand against the régime. Once again it was a time characterised by difficult decisions made in the desperate struggle for survival. The difference was that our decisions were now conditioned by ever-deteriorating circumstances. When death becomes imminent, decisions are made that, years later, you would rather forget. That journey to Belsen demonstrated to me the heights to which man, including myself, can soar and the depths to which he can plunge.

It did not start off that way. At first the journey gave me the chance to become better acquainted with one particular German guard who had adopted me in Wüsegiersdorf.

Helmut was a well-built and strong-looking man of about thirty. His small nose looked out of proportion to his broad, open face, but what drew me to Helmut were his gentle green eyes; in them I saw a familiar glimmer of humanity. Standing apart from the other guards, looking somewhat out of place, it appeared as if he were merely acting a role.

The first time I came across him was late one night, just after I had arrived in Wüsegiersdorf in the summer of 1944. Lying in my bunk, I desperately needed the toilet, but did not want to use the urination bucket on my floor. I went down the three floors of the block to go outside and was immediately accosted by this young soldier. He looked as surprised to see me as I was to see him. Grabbing his rifle from his shoulder he shouted, '*Du kannst nicht ausgehen*' [You can't go outside]. Pointing at me with his rifle he commanded, 'Use the bucket'. At first I was so bewildered that I could not understand him. Eventually, I realised that he was telling me to go back inside. However, despite the threatening, there seemed to be something soft about this guard who pointed his gun and struggled to maintain his authority. I therefore decided to look him straight in the eye; underneath his bravado I liked what I saw.

The second time I encountered him was some weeks later on one of our Sunday cultural evenings. During these nights the prisoners on the third floor would gather to listen to stories told by the older men, some of whom held high office, including government posts, like Vazsonyi. We also made music, using improvised instruments or using our voices to mimic the sound of an instrument.

I had made a trumpet out of an anti-Semitic poster that I

picked up from a street in Charlottenbrün, and was using this one Sunday as we were making music to mimic the horn solo in Tchaikovsky's Fifth Symphony when, suddenly, a prisoner shouted from the ground floor, 'Look out! There's a guard coming!'

We scurried to our beds, expecting trouble. The guards generally did not come into the blocks; this was the domain of the kapos. Landing on my bunk, I propped myself up on my elbows to see what would happen while the other prisoners threw the blankets over their heads and adopted various postures of sleep. Within seconds all was quiet.

As my bunk was practically at the top of the stairs at the entrance to our floor, I was able to peer down the winding staircase. The sound of the outside door banging shut echoed up through the floors, then the noise of stairs creaking as they strained under the weight of the intruder. Staring down into the darkness, the form of the guard, slowly ascending, became perceptible. For a moment I thought it was Schwartz himself and was about to disappear under my blanket when I saw the outline of a rifle on the man's shoulders and realised that it was only one of the ordinary guards.

With my heart pounding, I let go of my blanket and decided to try to size him up. His head and shoulders eventually emerged from the gloom and, looking up, his eyes instantly met mine. Purposefully, I scrutinised Helmut's not unfriendly face. He smiled faintly; was it a cynical calmness before the storm?

'Who's got the trumpet?' he demanded. His voice was strong and deep.

I was taken aback by his question and looked at him quizzically. He repeated it more forcefully, 'I asked you a question. *Wer hat die Trompete gespielt?*'

'Me,' I confessed, gathering myself together.

'Where have you hidden it?' he said reaching for my blanket in order to search the bunk. 'Give it here.'

'But I don't have a trumpet,' I quickly explained.

'Don't make me angry,' he warned. 'Just give it to me.'

From under my blanket I reluctantly brought out my trumpet: a rolled-up paper tube. 'This is my trumpet,' I declared and offered it up to him.

'For heaven's sake,' he murmured, staring disbelievingly at the offending instrument. Wearily he turned and went back down the stairs.

During the next evening's roll-call Helmut recognised me. He was off duty now and stood back from the rest of the troops, leaning against the wall of a building. He looked much younger, different from the rest. He kept glancing in my direction, gave me a reassuring smile and it seemed obvious that he wanted to talk to me. When we were dismissed he walked over, almost casually. He asked my name – this time with a soft, friendly voice.

'I have no name, now I am only a number, but I used to be called Ernest.'

'I am Helmut and I am not a Nazi,' he stated. 'Are you a musician?'

His conversational manner confounded me.

'No. A singer,' I hesitantly explained, not knowing quite what to make of him. Just then, another guard came towards us from across the Appelplatz and Helmut, realising how hazardous such an exchange was, furtively looked at our unwelcome audience and muttered reassuringly, 'We'll talk later.' Then, before hastily walking away, I felt his hand deposit something in my pocket. Somewhat surprised, I returned to my block, found a quiet corner and reached into my pocket. Two big, flat sugar lumps nestled against each other; I broke off one corner for myself and the rest I divided between my cousin Leopold and Walter, telling them about Helmut, 'You'll see. He's a Mensch.'

Over the next six months, until Wüsegiersdorf was evacuated, Helmut and I got to know each other a bit better through snatches of stolen conversation. I suspected that he had been drawn into the army against his wishes: in the Wehrmacht there were many others like Helmut – conscripts who were not ideologically committed to the régime.

My suspicions about Helmut were proved correct, he hated the régime, he hated the rest of the guards. But he felt powerless to do anything – perhaps having close contact with one of the prisoners was the catalyst he needed to begin to take a more active stand against the system. Now he was acquainted with an individual human being and not simply one of the despised, grey mass which he had been ordered to guard.

The morning we left Wüsegiersdorf, Helmut nonchalantly passed by and in a low voice instructed me to stay as close to him as possible. 'That way I'll be able to keep an eye on you. Remember to keep close to the rear of the column,' he enjoined me. 'The others won't be able to see when I pass you food.'

This plan was not always to prove feasible because, as the march continued, we were joined by groups of evacuated prisoners from other camps. It was sometimes difficult for Helmut to find me in the confusion.

Throughout the march I also kept close to a prisoner called Joe Lorinz, a boy whom I'd become friendly with after Walter's departure for Grossrozen. He was the only real friend I had left among the prisoners. When we left Wüsegiersdorf, my cousin Leopold and Zoltan had been designated to the group heading for Flossenburg. At the exact moment of our departure from the camp, Leopold had run over and, grabbing hold of me, thrust about eight chocolate drops into my pocket. I kept Leopold's parting gift as a treasure.

Joe and I were to become each other's lifeline during the course of the march: whatever Helmut gave to me, I gave to Joe – we were one and that is how we survived. Friendship was a key factor in survival, many times it was the encouragement of a friend that gave you something to fight, and indeed live, for.

Coming from a labour camp we had the advantage of being better fed than most of the other prisoners who joined us during the journey. But better fed only meant relatively better fed because all the prisoners on these journeys, which have become known as 'death marches', were suffering from malnutrition as well as disease and, after just a few days, we were not so much walking as dragging ourselves.

At first we were marched through the Silesian highlands where the snow and sleet drove perpetually down on us. After our first few months at Wüsegiersdorf we had been given civilian trousers and jackets instead of the striped 'pyjamas' in which we had arrived from Auschwitz. These garments afforded us some protection against the elements, but the real boon was that we had exchanged our wooden shoes for proper ones which helped enormously. Still, we possessed no heavy coats.

The guards on each side of the column looked on as we dragged ourselves day after day through the mud, snow and ice. We spent our nights in the open. The feeble and ill failed to get up in the morning or fell by the wayside during the day.

The march must have lasted for a little over two weeks. About five days into the march, a group of roughly a hundred women of all ages joined us. They looked starved and their heads were covered by coarse blankets. They were kept at a distance of approximately fifty yards behind our group and guarded by vicious-looking female SS. We had no idea who they were or where they had come from – they looked pathetic, an awful sight. But, despite their circumstances, they still tried to maintain a semblance of dignity: for example, when any woman needed the toilet a circle of women would form, providing a barrier against the eyes of onlookers.

Looking behind me at these unfortunate women, I saw a young, beautiful girl in the front row. What was more, she was looking at me. My heart stopped as I thought I recognised the face of my first love – Medy.

I had not seen Medy since that spring morning in 1942, when I noticed her in a group of girls in front of the synagogue in Budapest, but I had often dreamed about her. In the camps I used to imagine her Greta Garbo profile and soft hair before I fell asleep in my bunk. I pulled the blanket over my head and concentrated all my thoughts on her. That was my favourite nightly routine: just seeing her.

'What is it?' inquired Joe, as I stared behind me at the column of bedraggled women.

'I think I know that girl.'

'Which one?'

I furtively gestured, saying, 'That one there, the taller one in the front row.' Joe's eyes found her.

'Please, let it be Medy,' I prayed. Then immediately I wondered what on earth I could do even if it was her. What if they changed direction? What if I could not make contact? And even if I did, how could I begin to help her?

Then I remembered the eight chocolate sweets that Leopold had given me at the gate of Wüsegiersdorf that were still waiting quietly in my pocket. Explaining the situation to Joe, I decided to give two sweets to the girl: 'I'll pretend to tie my shoelaces and stay behind.'

'They'll never fall for that one,' replied Joe.

I ignored him. 'I'll give her the chocolates and then run back.'

'It'll be a miracle if you ever do make it back, Ernest, let's think about this for a minute.'

'Joe, there's no time to think. It'll be dark soon. Who knows what will happen? They might even go off in the opposite direction.'

'All right. Let's try it,' he finally said, resolutely.

With the sweets in my hand and my heart pounding, I gradually fell behind the rest of my group. Bending down, I fiddled with my laces. In a few moments I would see Medy or be shot.

From the corner of my eye I saw the feet of the anonymous women trudging towards me. The front row of their column was nearly level with my crouched body. I stood up and glanced in the girl's direction, her big blue eyes were looking at me, she was waiting – her hand outstretched towards mine. I peered hopefully into her eyes – it was not Medy.

All I could do was drop the two sweets into her palm and turn away to sprint back to Joe. Just then I noticed one of the female guards racing towards me. 'What do you think you're doing, you piece of filth!' Her boot landed full on my backside, sending me flying into the air. From nearby I heard Helmut shouting at her, 'You miserable cow!'

'Don't tell me you feel sorry for a Jew?' she screamed back at him, disbelievingly. By drawing the female guard's attention, Helmut had given me the chance to race back to Joe.

After about three days the group of women prisoners disappeared. From that time, moving on became very difficult as the weather deteriorated with snow and ice making walking practically impossible. The little food we had saved was long forgotten and a few days went by without fresh water or sustenance. Many gave up, sitting down beside the road, unable to continue. So weak that not even the threat of being shot could convince them to go on.

The weather was practically relentless when the guards suddenly halted the march. After a moment's conference we were herded towards a village called Kwalish. The group was then split up and the group I was in was led up to a cluster of farm buildings away to our left. It was here that we were to witness another example of real human kindness in the form of Max, a German farmer.

His farm was situated on a plateau on the hillside. On the right, as we walked in, was the actual farmhouse – a long low building. On the left there were some huts which the guards requisitioned for their own shelter. Straight ahead of us was a small wooden barn with a loft which looked big enough to hold about fifty people.

There were, however, about two hundred of us and we were all to be locked up in that barn. There was no light and no heating, but at least we were sheltered from the weather. As we were marched into the barn we saw a tall, well-built man in his early sixties with a big oval face and high cheekbones. He was wearing boots and a cap, talking earnestly with the guards.

We later learned the farmer was called Max. He had a big deep voice, and there was something reminiscent of Anton in him. Like the small workshop master, the farmer certainly was not overly impressed by the German uniforms which had descended upon him.

The conversation between Max and the guards was becoming quite heated. Even though we could hear only fragments of what he was saying, we sensed that we were going to get something from this farmer. When we heard Max utter the word '*Kartoffel*', we realised that he was negotiating with the guards to be allowed to give us potatoes.

By that time potatoes were a luxury in comparison with the food rations we received. The last time I had eaten potatoes was at home in Budapest – in the camps you were lucky if you found a piece of potato in the soup.

To us a potato was a delicacy full of wonderful flavours and nourishment. While the weather conditions made it impossible for us to leave the farm for another ten days, Max handed out to each of us a whole boiled potato from a huge metal drum, as we lined up at about three or four o'clock every afternoon. He even threw some potatoes away because they were judged either too small or too rotten to be given out.

Being outnumbered by the soldiers, Max was hardly in a secure position, still, he was not going to obey their orders. There was one incident where some of the prisoners saw Max getting into such a rage with one of the guards that he kicked the soldier square on the backside.

He appeared quite a stubborn character, obviously believing that the Nazis were just a passing affliction that had to be endured – like a bout of bad weather, or a mildewed harvest – the storm-clouds would not stay forever; the next season would be better. From what little we learned about Max, he appeared to be a religious man who believed that God would reward him in his afterlife for the humanity he showed towards his fellow beings.

By now, I had become sceptical about religion. Even if the Nazis were defeated, could any of us really return to 'normality'? Some illusions had been irreparably damaged – God for one. Despite Max's attitude, this feeling grew stronger while staying on the farm.

During the day we were allowed out of the barn and I saw a guard throwing a sardine tin away; making sure that no one was watching, I went over and picked it up. Sadly, there was no fish left, only oil. Then I dried out some string I had found trapped in the ice, and made the sardine tin into a lamp and, after some unsuccessful attempts, the wick was finally lit. Back in the barn that night, a group of us sat around the little flame and spontaneously started the Chanukah tune, *Maoz Tzur* – the festival had taken place several months earlier. I thought back to my reunion with Leopold in Wüsegiersdorf when we had both been praying: now, as I prayed again, there was a hollow feeling in my soul as I merely mouthed the words. Looking at our makeshift lamp, I saw that it was just a reminder of a childish belief; a faith I had known as a boy in Bratislava; a faith to which I could never return. Since November 1938 my relationship with God had undergone serious challenges but this journey had still more to offer.

After ten days on the farm we moved on. Naturally, we scanned the area for a glimpse of Max before our departure but he could not be seen. This struck us as strange because he was usually in the vicinity, so we wondered if his flagrant disregard for the guards' authority had cost him dear. Just as we were leaving the courtyard, a woman – the farmer's wife or perhaps his daughter – stood outside the farmhouse door. Her sudden presence was a complete surprise to us as, for all of those ten days we had not even suspected she existed. From the doorway she shouted: 'I should have given you two potatoes a day.' Over the noise and clatter one of the prisoners shouted back: 'Never mind, you saved our lives.'

~ • ~

We were crossing into lowland country when we marched into a small village, possibly a suburb of Dessau. It was late afternoon and the snow was coming down harder than ever before. The guards halted the march and exchanged a few

~

words. We were then marched to a building on the other side of the village, isolated from the other houses; it was either a warehouse or some sort of industrial building with a corrugated roof. The guards began pushing us inside with their hands and the butts of their rifles. I looked around for Helmut but could not see him.

This building could hold about eighty people at the most but, by now, there were about four hundred of us. More and more people were pushed in and we were no longer standing but falling over each other. People began screaming for help: '*Deutsche Wehrmacht, hilfe!*'

The call for help was unanswered, instead we heard the door being shut and bolts slid across the outside. Realising that we were locked in with no means of escape, fear turned to immediate panic and a stampede ensued just like cattle in a corral. And animals we certainly became, climbing on top of each other, using our fists, feet and teeth – it was almost like swimming in a sea of writhing bodies as hands and feet fought to keep heads afloat as in the waters of deep and stormy seas. As the night progressed the building became like a mincer: bodies became mattresses, layer upon layer, and those underneath were crushed to death.

All through that long night Joe and I tried to stay together, fight together – whatever we did, we did together. Many times we were on the verge of giving up, believing we had no hope for survival, but animal instinct won. That night I learned the uncompromising truth that, in those circumstances, you cling to life and fight – even if it meant pushing down someone else. In that situation it was either kill or be killed; moral soul-searching did not enter the equation.

About four hundred of us had entered that building; about 100 never left. I did not look behind at the dead and dying as the doors were flung open the next morning. The previous few hours had left me half-crazed, I was only interested in myself and Joe. It was only afterwards, years later, that the impact of that night hit me and today I still suffer with guilt for having survived at the expense of others. Images of people drowning in an ocean of bodies, shouting for help, pushed under by the stronger – myself included – will always haunt me.

As Joe and I emerged from the building, lo and behold we were given a small piece of bread with a dollop of butter on it. It was a surreal moment after what had just happened. For many that would be the last morsel of food before arriving at Belsen.

We left and marched on for only half an hour to Dessau railway station where we were herded onto open cattle trucks. Other groups of evacuated prisoners had joined the column by then, so there must have been at least 1,500 people in total. I wearily helped Joe up into one of the overcrowded trucks.

'Ernest!'

Some bread flew through the air. Helmut had been running down the platform with this half loaf of bread which I now caught in my hands. Unfortunately, the starving mob around me immediately tore it away in a wild frenzy; they hardly left me a mouthful in my clenched fist. But for Helmut to find me in that swarm of people was an amazing feat in itself.

The snow had been falling all day when our train drew to a halt near a tall white station building at Aussig on the river Elbe. The snow was lying on the few thin blankets that the eighty or ninety prisoners in my wagon had to share. In an attempt to generate heat and comfort, they constantly wriggled like dying worms in a can. The situation was made worse after more prisoners were pushed onto our already overcrowded wagon. The new arrivals were infested with lice and we soon felt the repercussions of their unwelcome presence.

The sky became clear and we could see the station building, shining in the moonlight, reflected in the river. It was bitterly cold – our breath froze as it hung in the air. In the corner of the wagon was a stool, reserved for the guard, sometimes Helmut, sometimes another soldier. Around midnight Helmut climbed onto the wagon and took up his position on the stool. I sat next to him while Joe lay a bit further away, between us lay a Polish man who softly spoke in Yiddish with his two teenage sons.

Helmut immediately saw that I was clutching my stomach. 'What's the matter?' He was bending over me and I saw the concern etched in his face.

'Diarrhoea – I don't know – something's not right,' I muttered as another spasm hit me and I doubled up in pain. 'I have to go,' and I reached out a limp arm and tried to get up.

'Here, let me help.' And Helmut put his arms under mine and lifted me to my feet.

'Please, Helmut, I can manage,' I protested, feeling thoroughly humiliated at the position I had been reduced to.

'You're sick – you've got the strength of a baby. No argument.'

He was right. My strength was seeping out of me with the contents of my intestines. Helping me to sit over the edge of the wagon, he asked, 'Can you manage?' Receiving no answer he got up himself to support my weight.

'Really, Helmut, you don't have to do this,' I implored him.

He simply looked me in the eye and said, 'Yes, I do. I can see you're suffering hell. Now, just go.' More diarrhoea was released from my body. After a moment Helmut helped me back into the wagon. He was to do the same all over again every twenty minutes or so when the attacks returned all through that pitiless cold night.

'Thank you, Helmut,' I murmured as I collapsed back onto

the floor. 'I don't think even my own brother would have done that for me.'

After a moment Helmut asked, 'Do you have a brother?' We had never spoken of our families before and I told him about my brothers and sisters, my parents and how my father had raised us in a strictly orthodox Jewish tradition. He listened eagerly and then said: 'After all this, all this misery, do you still believe that there is a God?'

I did not answer.

'I had a brother,' Helmut said after a moment.

'Dead?'

Helmut nodded.

'In the army?' I continued.

'No. Joseph was never in the army. He had lost one of his eyes in an accident when he was young. He never did seem to have much luck.' Then he laughed, adding, 'Quite a family, mine. My father lost a leg when he was younger too. I can picture them both now – my father with his artificial leg and my brother with his glass eye. Still, my father was a dentist, so at least we always had good teeth in our family.'

He seemed amused at this bizarre image but then looked at me and suddenly seemed much older. 'I ask you about God because, you see, He was also important in our house. But religion brought nothing but misery, argument. I think it was even responsible for Joseph's death.' He looked away angrily. '*Mit der Religion bin ich fertig* [I've had it with religion].'

'How did Joseph die?'

'He killed himself.'

I hesitated, then pressed on. 'Why?' I asked softly.

'Perhaps because he was in love – that's what my father believes. But really it was my mother who killed him: her and her love for the Holy Virgin Mary and the Nazis. She cannot get enough of either of them. And Hitler?' He shuddered. 'She is crazy about him. *Ganz verrückt mit dem Führer* [Totally in love with the man].'

'What about your father? Is he religious?'

'No, not at all.' He smiled to himself. 'Every Sunday morning while Mother went to chapel with her friends, my father was with his friends having a game of cards. He loves cards. He never takes any notice of Mother's sermonising. And he certainly has no respect for her political views either.'

'Was Joseph a Nazi?'

'No. He was always a very sensitive boy – prone to depression. So, of course, he was inevitably the type to fall in love, fatally . . .'

Helmut continued, driven on by some unfathomable desire to tell his brother's story: 'Helga was her name. My sisters told me that she was very beautiful. A petite, blonde doll of a girl. Czech. You see, we come from the Sudetenland, where many Czech people live.

'I never met the girl myself as I was in the army by then. It wasn't until I came home on leave that my father took me to one side and told me about Joseph's death. I couldn't believe it.' He stopped for a moment. He was breathing rapidly. I placed my hand on his shoulder.

'Helga's father was a widowed watchmaker,' Helmut continued, recovering himself. 'But he was also in the Resistance – or so they said. Anyway, he was hauled in by the Gestapo and Helga was naturally also under suspicion. She had to hide. So she turned to Joseph. What else could she do? Joseph went to Father who was sympathetic, but he pointed out that Mother would probably have none of it. In fact, she would be the first one to denounce the poor girl. What could they do? Well, my ather decided that the best thing to do would be to temporarily hide

Helga in the shed at the bottom of the garden until they could find her a more permanent hiding place. Joseph would make inquiries into a suitable location for her to hide out, and meanwhile my father dragged out some blankets and one of his old coats and tried to make the girl as comfortable as possible.'

'All the while your mother didn't know what was going on?' I asked.

'No, she was too busy with her friends at the chapel to be bothered with what was happening at home. Joseph would sneak down to the bottom of the garden and take food to Helga when no one was looking.'

'So, what went wrong?'

'After about three days, Joseph went to the shed to tell Helga they had found her a place, but she'd gone. There was a note on the door. She had sneaked out into the street and met a girl from the Resistance and Helga was asked to join them. They would help her to hide and she accepted. She wrote that this meant that as Joseph was a German she couldn't see him any more. Well, my brother was devastated. He worshipped that girl. My father said that Joseph became very withdrawn and wouldn't eat. Eventually, he just killed himself.'

There was a long silence and then Helmut added: 'You see, if only my mother hadn't been so in love with the Führer and with God, then none of this would have happened. Helga wouldn't have been driven away and Joseph wouldn't have committed suicide. You know, I even believe that Joseph did it to spite our mother, to make her suffer for everything she believed in.'

Then Helmut looked at me wearily and said, 'That's why I've had it with religion.' Turning aside, he looked at the people moaning in the wagon. 'For us, Ernest, the war is lost,' Helmut sighed. 'And yet the killing goes on. Look at all this senseless

121

suffering around us. What is it all for? I never could have believed such carnage and agony was possible.'

'I've seen worse,' I offered and, as I looked him in the eye, I told him about Auschwitz, about the gassing, about the stench of burning bodies.

He remained silent, absolutely stunned and said at last: 'We are actually doing that to the world? I can't believe it.' Then he added again: 'I've had it with religion. We must realise that God has no influence on events. He doesn't even lift a finger and our prayers are useless.' He sighed deeply. 'I've had it with religion,' he repeated. As I looked at him I thought back to the makeshift Chanukah lamp in the barn on Max's farm and admitted wearily, 'I have too.'

We were silent for a bit. Then Helmut pointed at the shivering figures in the wagon again and asked who would benefit from all the senseless suffering; 'That's the German people for you. And here am I, in a German uniform, and what can I do?'

But in his own way Helmut had done a lot. The way he cared for me that night proved that he was different from his comp-atriots. He stood apart from the killing machine. His brother's suicide as a result of his mother's zealous love of Hitler and religion obviously played a part in his attitude. Moreover, his friendship with me made him analyse the political situation and its consequent human suffering more deeply than most Germans did. But, even before the incident with Helga and Joseph, Helmut had been different. From the way he talked about his father I could tell there was an immense depth of love and respect between them. The father had not been fooled by the Nazi propaganda and probably warned his son not to get involved with it. Both Helmut and I shared a moral code that we had inherited from our fathers. 'Just be a Mensch,' my father had told me and Helmut was a Mensch. With more people like him, much suffering could have been prevented. Unfortunately, there were many willing murderers. But it is important to remember that not every German was swept along by the political tide.

Yet, Helmut's rebellion against the régime was to extend even further when he was confronted with the appalling sight that greeted us on arrival at Bergen-Belsen. There Helmut did something that did not affect the course of the war in any way, but as a gesture was extraordinary.

It must have been about two o'clock in the morning when our train arrived at the unloading ramp of Belsen. We immediately noticed a figure roaring and screaming, lashing out in every direction with a gigantic whip. This was Joseph Kramer, the camp commandant. He looked like a great ox of a man, standing there in his long leather coat with his collar up against the cold. We were lined up on the ramp to march to the camp which was at some distance from the station.

The guards around us were shivering, cursing and kicking, as we walked along a tree-lined avenue towards the camp. That path became a graveyard, as those who were too weak or ill fell under our feet and those who refused to get up were shot. The father who had been lying beside Joe in the wagon pleaded with his two sons in Yiddish: 'Children, please, please, let me go.' They continued to try to drag him along, encouraging him not to give up. Then, amidst hysterical sobbing, they finally had to abandon him. The old man fell and he was trampled to death by those behind him. We were walking on a carpet of bodies. Like in the barn outside Dessau I walked on the bodies of others, determined to continue the struggle to survive.

We arrived at the gates of Belsen. An icy wind howled over the flat landscape and mixed with the growling and barking of the guards and dogs. Miraculously, Helmut managed to find me in the dark, in all that confusion. He had made the effort to find me amongst the thousands of other prisoners, while running the risk of being seen by the other guards. He opened his flask and told me to drink. My mouth was filthy, but it did not matter to Helmut, nor did it matter to him when I immediately passed it to my friend Joe. Helmut also produced some bread with grease on it.

Then Kramer suddenly reappeared and selected ten able men to return with him to the station ramp to clear the wagons of the dead and dying. I was pointed out but the frightening thought of being separated from my friend Joe made me hesitate. Desperately, I tried to make eye contact with Joe when a terrible pain stopped me in my tracks: Kramer's whip had landed right across my face. My right cheek swelled up immediately like a sausage and I was convinced that I had lost my right eye forever.

Back on the ramp, several lorries were already heaped up with bodies. Through the cursing and yammering came Kramer's voice: 'Do you hear? Matchsticks. I want them piled up like matchsticks!'

When I looked around, I saw Helmut standing motionless in the middle of all this confusion; he had a look of complete disbelief on his face. Like a lost child, he appeared totally engrossed and paralysed by the scene he was witnessing. Kramer spotted him too and went over shouting: 'You idiot, what are you doing, standing there?'

Helmut just stared Kramer in the face. And then slowly and deliberately he took his rifle from his shoulder and pointed it at Belsen's commandant. The other guards were unable to move; was this soldier really going to kill the commandant? Was his gun loaded? By the determined expression on Helmut's face, and the way he was purposefully grasping the rifle, he looked as though he was going to shoot.

We all remained silent for a few more moments, until Kramer judged the situation correctly and recovered. The commandant laughed and said in front of the other guards, 'Don't worry, I'll get you later.' And then he walked off, clearly very amused. Helmut lowered his rifle and, looking my way, we caught each other's eye. It was a deeply humiliating moment for Helmut – to have Kramer just walk away, deflating the heroism of Helmut's gesture – but I felt enormously proud of my German guard. That picture of Helmut pointing his rifle at Joseph Kramer on the ramp was my last sight of him.

~ • ~

When I was in Budapest in the early 1950s, the famous singer Dietrich Fischer-Dieskau gave a recital. As soon as he stepped on stage it was as if Helmut was standing in front of me – that same friendly face. I was transported back to the night on the Elbe when I told Helmut that I came from a long line of singers and that if I survived the nightmare I, too, would like to follow in the family tradition. He put his hand on my shoulder and said, 'You'll make it.' He was always saying that to me, encouraging me not to give up. Then he added, 'If I could sing I would give half my life away.' Then he quoted an adage which I remembered my mother also saying:

Wo dass Singen ist, dort lasse dich nieder
Böse Leute haben keine Lieder

Which freely translated is:

Where there is singing, there you should dwell
Wicked people have no songs to tell

Helmut was right. I survived, but without Helmut these things would never have come to pass. Without him I would not be alive today. How many other anonymous and unpraised Germans like Helmut enabled people like myself to gaze down at our own grandchildren? I have never forgotten Helmut and not a day goes by when I do not think about him and wish him well, wherever he may be. And there lies much regret, for I have never been able to track him down. As with so many other people, I never asked his second name.

Looking at my grandchildren I am also reminded that I survived because one night outside Dessau my feet and hands kept me afloat in an ocean of bodies, pushing others to their deaths. Nothing is ever clear-cut. Perhaps my simple gesture of giving two chocolate sweets to an anonymous girl gave her the encouragement she needed to carry on. I will never know. One act does not cancel out the other, they are not even related. It shows, however, that a person is never truly evil or completely good. Your life can never really be evaluated as if it were merely an account book of moral debits and credits.

That night outside Dessau also proved to me that it is pointless to try and predict your own behaviour. Given a particular situation you think you know how your conscience would compel you to act, but between the thought and the act lies an abyss called pragmatism: the urge to live. What makes a man retain his humanity and what turns him into a beast? All I know is what I have witnessed: examples of the greatest heroism and the ultimate human degradation – the heights and the depths of man. Of that, who could dare judge?

6

ARRIVAL IN HELL

~

Day began to break as the lorry took us back to Bergen-Belsen and, as the truck drove through a gate, I had my first full view of Belsen. Behind an endless row of wooden barracks the horizon was glowing red, as if an enormous fire was raging. In that early-morning light, shadowy figures in the camp, skeletons wrapped in blankets, shuffled almost aimlessly in slow motion. It seemed as if they were heading towards the first roll-call of the day. Then, suddenly, one of the bodies in the lorry sat upright against the glowing red sky and said in a clear voice, 'My name is Dr Weiss. I am a physician from Budapest.' As soon as he had said it, he fell back and never moved again. Dr Weiss would not be attending roll-call.

When the lorry came to a halt, I slid down quickly and stumbled into the first barracks I came to. My only thought was to hide from the inferno outside, find a corner of a bunk and get some rest.

'Ernest?' a voice enquired disbelievingly from across the hut. It was Joe. He threw his arms around me. The other prisoners watched us impassively as we could hardly contain our joy.

Compared to the other inmates, Joe and I must have looked relatively fit and when, a few days after our arrival, a group was selected to clear rubble in the nearby town, we were chosen. We were happy to leave, even if it was only temporarily.

The town we were marched to was Hildesheim. Allied bombs had destroyed the railway station there, and our job was to dislodge a railway carriage that had disappeared down a crater. As we began to dig through the rubble it became apparent that no provision had been made to supply us with water or food. Not having anything to eat was not that bad. We soon discovered that the carriage was loaded with butter and cream. Our spades cut through layers of debris and butter – it looked just like layers of a cake, a beautiful birthday cake – and we scraped the butter from our spades to eat it. Unfortunately, the day wore on and no water appeared and the salty butter made us even more thirsty.

The extreme thirst triggered off a kind of madness, and I lost my head completely. Not caring if any of the guards was looking, I ran into the station building hoping to find something to drink. Like a madman I ran from room to room. In the basement I could not believe my luck: crates with glass bottles. I lifted one, only to find it empty. Hundreds of bottles were sitting there bone-dry in their crates.

Running again, I suddenly found myself in an enormous kitchen. Two women turned round as I rushed in. Both were no longer young, one must have been at least fifty years old, while the other was already in her sixties. They were dressed in pinnies, standing at a big, old-fashioned stone sink where they were washing pans. The dishwater was as thick as sludge but I made a dash for that sink and, pushing the two women away, thrust my face into the filthy water. '*Nein, nein, nein!*' the women screamed, trying to haul me away; '*Du darfst das nicht*! [You mustn't do that!]'

At that point the noise of heavy boots reverberated down the steps. The women exchanged looks with each other and then they stared at my 'pyjamas'. The younger froze, not knowing what to do. But the elder one, realising what was happening, immediately pulled me towards a cupboard and tried to stuff me in before I could say a word. Seeing that there was not enough room, she pulled me away and pushed me behind a washing line on which an assortment of clothes and towels were hanging. Throwing some more aprons and towels on the line, she managed to create a protective screen just as the soldiers broke in.

'Where is he?' demanded one.

My heart was thundering. I heard the woman who had pushed me behind the clothes turning round and saying, as if in distress, 'Yes, we saw him. He went out the other door.' There was a fraction of a second's silence. 'Quick, you must hurry,' she added. The sound of boots on flagstones receded.

'You can come out now,' said my quick-thinking saviour.

I left my hiding place. '*Dankeschön*,' I said in a daze.

'All right,' she said, not quite sure what to do next, 'disappear!' and she made a gesture with her arms.

'Wait,' the younger one said and, producing an earthenware mug from the cupboard, poured me a good measure of fruit juice. It tasted like raspberries. She smiled shyly at the way I was enjoying it. Gulping it quickly I thanked the two women again and scurried back to Joe and the rest of my unit.

~ • ~

There are people who at crucial moments do the right thing: their humanity shines through. Sometimes, when one person tries to do the right thing, it acts as an example to others and those watching cannot help but join in. That is what happened with those two women. The elder made a moral decision and the younger one followed her. But, more often than not, the reverse happened. One person committed an atrocity and others turned a blind eye or participated. This was brought vividly home to me by the events that followed the escape in the kitchen.

~ • ~

We had been billeted in an old theatre in Hildesheim when the town was attacked by a second Allied air-strike. It was mid-afternoon on a Friday when the air-raid sirens rang out. As we ran out of the theatre we found the streets were filled with people trying to flee from the city. Bombs exploded around us and the ground moved as if an earthquake was taking place. In the panic and confusion some of the prisoners inevitably mounted the pavement – it was absolutely forbidden for prisoners to do that.

On the opposite side of the street a one-legged soldier leaning on his crutches started screaming: '*Lass doch die Juden nicht am Gehsteig* [Don't let the Jews on to the pavement].'

I shouted back with all my strength: '*Maul halten, du idiot* [Shut up, you idiot].'

The soldier's eyes widened in complete disbelief. Amidst the destruction and danger his only thought was to maintain Aryan dominance.

That afternoon Hildesheim was completely destroyed. Flames leapt from the window of the theatre where we had been housed and, with no shelter left, we had to move on. We were marched to Hannover-Ahlem, a relatively small camp, where we were put to work in an underground mine. It was to be ten days of sheer hell before we were sent back to Belsen.

The Germans were excavating the mine and converting it into a munitions factory that would be hundreds of feet away from the surface and, presumably, safe from aerial attacks. The race was on to get it finished as soon as possible and so we were brought in. It was an insane situation. The Germans must have known that the war was lost but here they were, in March 1945, building an underground factory to aid the war effort.

My unit worked the night shift. As we went down in the lift we would see the other prisoners coming up. The majority of them were Dutchmen and unused to manual labour. They looked like walking dead – pale phantoms rather than living humans.

Many of the corridors in the mine were about head-high, no more, and about the width of a narrow lane. Water dripped incessantly down the rock face and it was bitterly cold – our hands soon became icicles. By the iron rails which ran throughout the works were alcoves where you could shield yourself. The constant explosions, used to enlarge the mine more rapidly, filled the air with viscous smoke and dust. For many minutes after each explosion, work ground to a halt as we tried to catch our breath.

One evening, as I was clearing away some debris, a guard in his early twenties, about my height and build, came up to me: 'C'mon, put your back into it.'

'Yes, sir,' I replied in German and risking another comment added, 'This section shouldn't take too long now,'

'How come you speak such good German?'

'We always spoke German at home,' I replied, hoping to

engage him in conversation to get on his good side. He was young and lost-looking, a bit like Helmut. I thought he might be worth the risk.

'And where was home?' he enquired.

My gamble seemed to be paying off. 'Bratislava,' I ventured.

'No?' he said, astonished. 'I'm from Bratislava too. Did you ever go and see the football?'

'Sure,' I replied.

'Which team did you support?'

'SK Bratislava.'

'Me too,' he said.

As we chatted away about our mutual interests, he took his rifle from his shoulder and leant it against the wall. Behind him, a small Jew, Mr Klein, whom I knew from Budapest, was coming our way with a wheelbarrow full of rubble. He was trying hard to control the heavy load but, being too small and frail, he found the task very difficult. Just then a taller and older guard hove into sight and surveyed the scene. By now we had learned that this other guard was a brute of a man. He looked disapprovingly at his compatriot engaging in what must have appeared a fairly genial conversation with a prisoner.

Suddenly, Klein lost control of the wheelbarrow and rammed it into my guard's legs. The soldier turned round furiously but, seeing Klein cowering in terror, he did not know quite what to do. The older guard then laughed at the younger man. My guard turned red.

'*Was willst du denn mit dem kleinen Jude machen?* [What are you going to do with your small Jew?]'

The young guard just looked at the elder one.

'*Ich wundere mich* [I wonder],' he continued. All the prisoners in the tunnel were now staring at the young guard and a terrified Klein.

Then the elder guard finally said, '*Erschlag ihm*! [Kill him!]'

Only then, the younger one slapped Klein on the face. But the elder just laughed and said, 'Nein, erschlag ihm! Erschlag ihm!'

My guard began hitting Klein from all sides, the older guard egging him on. In a rage, the younger man picked up his rifle and beat Klein about the head with the butt. As Klein fell to the floor, I moved away. I could not believe it: one minute this young guard was talking to me like a fellow human being and the next he was behaving like an animal, just because he had been goaded on by another. My last glimpse of the scene was Klein's inert body being dumped into his wheelbarrow by other prisoners and taken away.

Herd mentality was crucial in Nazi Germany: everyone was always watching someone else, judging how they reacted to certain situations, whilst afraid of being denounced themselves. The younger Germans were brought up under a dictatorship, their behaviour pattern inculcated by Nazi ideology. They had not only been taught to obey orders without question, but to behave in the manner expected of them. On his own the younger guard could be himself but as soon as another German was there he reverted to his Nazi mentality. The younger woman in the Hildesheim kitchen had done the opposite. Encouraged by her compatriot to do the right thing, she had helped me to survive a little longer. It was so typical: one German on his own was relatively predictable, but add another to the equation and you could not predict what would happen. It brought out either the best or the worst in them.

About nine or ten days later we set out to return to Bergen-Belsen. We were met at the gate by a walking skeleton wrapped in a blanket. 'None of you will get out alive!' he screamed deliriously. 'The camp is infested with typhoid!'

One of the main problems in Belsen was the lack of fresh water; many resorted to drinking from puddles of dirty water into which ran excrement and urine. By the end of March 1945 thousands were dying every day. The death toll was exacerbated by contact with the infected dead. Those still living were forced to drag the dead towards open mass graves. That was my assignment after returning from Hannover-Ahlem.

We worked in teams around the clock. I got very friendly with a Romanian carpenter (Joe had by that time been moved to the Hungarian barracks) but there was never enough energy left for much conversation. The process of hauling bodies was exhausting business in our degraded and debilitated state.

Late one evening I had collapsed near the pit, unable to continue. When I awoke I realised I was alone. My Romanian friend had disappeared. Suddenly a young guard appeared from nowhere: 'Get into the pit!' he ordered, pointing his gun at me. 'Start pulling the bodies out from the edge into the centre.'

I mustered all my strength and slipped down into the pit, but the effort had drained me and I sat catatonic in the dirt among the dead.

'Do you hear me? Start moving the bodies!'

I fell onto my side, succumbing to fatigue. Realising that it was impossible for me to carry out his instructions the guard gave up. With his gun hanging lifelessly in his hand, he stared into the emptiness. My eyes closed and I drifted off; I felt sure that this was the end.

When I opened my eyes again it was night. In the moonlight I recognised a man sitting in an upright position to my right; it was my Romanian carpenter. His blue eyes seemed to be looking at me. I smiled and said, 'Let's get out of here.' He did not move. Thinking he was too tired, I begged him to move: 'Try to get up.' But he did not move an inch, then I realised he was dead. Death from starvation occurs with the eyes open.

It must have been human instinct to stay alive that made me try to ascend the pit walls once more. After several attempts I got to the edge of the pit and then clambered out. Lying there in the darkness, I slowly became aware of a lot of commotion. Lorries arrived one after another and guards began unloading hundreds of bodies. The Germans hurled the stiff cadavers into the pit. Then I noticed with a shock that the corpses were the bodies of young girls who still had all their hair and looked relatively well fed. They could not have been inmates from Belsen.

Then a sound to my left made me turn my head. A German soldier, in his fifties, leaning on his bike and unaware of my presence, was approached by a younger man, also with a bike. Lying still at the edge of the pit I could hear every word they said. 'Nice thing we've done here, eh?' said the younger, studying the view.

'What?' the older guard replied.

'Nice thing we've done to the world,' he repeated.

And the older one replied, 'Your awakening is pretty late.'

I never learned the identity of the girls, but the episode was typical: many Germans did not wake up until the killing was over and almost everyone was dead. Only now, as the inevitability of defeat loomed, did the Germans begin to question the wisdom of the Nazi system. Only now did they ask aloud what it had all been for. But, conversely, many merely redoubled their efforts. The insane fervour with which the building of the factory in Hannover-Ahlem was undertaken was characteristic of this hysteria. So were the comments of the one-legged soldier in Hildesheim, desperately clinging to an ideology and way of thought that was rapidly crumbling.

In the last few weeks of the war the Germans lost control

over the hundreds of camps and the guards who were meant to be running them. In Belsen the Germans began to disappear and with no personnel, no real organisation, thousands of prisoners were left at the mercy of the kapos and the Hungarian guards who had been brought in and who were left arming the machine-guns on the watch-towers. In the end there seemed to be hardly any Germans left. In reality, many Germans, aware of the approaching Allied troops, disappeared in the barracks. They hid in the uniforms of dead prisoners in order to escape justice. That was the ultimate disgrace of the German army. They now revealed themselves as cowards.

It was a maddening chaos. With no clean water the typhoid epidemic was now raging and thousands of people were in the grip of death. People lay dying in the dirt, among the piles of dead and the pools of excrement. One of the main symptoms of typhoid is dysentery and people relieved themselves where they could,

It did not yet mean the end of the beatings. During the last days a number of kapos clubbed a man to death. As he lay down on the ground next to me, with blood running from his open wounds, I tried to move away, but I was too tired.

'Serves him right,' muttered another prisoner lying near by.

'Why? What did he do?' asked another.

'He opened up the body of a dead man and started to eat the liver.'

Such was the level of starvation during those last few days.

Amidst all these things, Bergen-Belsen was liberated. Lying on the ground by a fence, succumbing to typhoid and unable to move, I saw military vehicles in the distance. As they drew closer it became apparent that they were not German. 'My God, it's the Allies!' somebody whispered.

At first nobody seemed to take any real notice. Many no

longer had the strength to move or care. A handful, however, managed to drag themselves to the fence. 'Are they American?' asked one wretch lying nearby. 'No, it's the British,' answered another voice. I remember very clearly lying back in the dirt and thinking, 'At last – it's over.'

But my personal suffering had not yet come to an end. The British troops liberated Belsen at the beginning of April 1945. It was a strangely quiet affair and many prisoners remained unaware that their saviours had arrived because it took such a long time for the British to actually drive into the camp: the roads were blocked with dead and dying. Their first job was to start clearing bodies. The British soldiers could not believe their eyes; many had seen atrocities fighting their way through Europe but stood overwhelmed at what they saw in Belsen. That it had been human beings who had inflicted such conditions on their fellow men was unfathomable.

Faced with thousands dying of disease, thirst and starvation, the British were faced with an impossible task, but they tried to arrange matters as quickly as possible. Water was brought to the camp by the fire brigades who connected hundreds of yards of hose. Now we had water, but there were not enough people to hand it out to the very ill. Many had to be helped on an individual basis by lifting up their heads and helping them to drink. Makeshift latrines were hastily established – because of the typhoid and other gastric disorders, your body was simply incapable of holding the food in your system – no sooner had you finished with the latrine than you needed it again. The British had built single-sex latrines, but we were beyond caring and just went to the ones that were the nearest. Many could not even make it to the latrines and just relieved themselves where they were sitting or squatting. The Tommies could not believe their eyes.

Just when I thought it was all over, I got an enormous shock. This concerned Medy, the girl I had fallen in love with in Dunajskza Streda and whom I still loved, although I had not seen her for years since, apart from that glimpse in Budapest.

To try and stem the raging epidemic, the British concentrated all those suffering from typhoid, including myself, in a single block of barracks. We were lying in a round formation and I was on the top bed of three bunks. Everyone was whimpering with high fever, thirst and dysentery. When you needed to go to the toilet you had to clamber down the bunks and run as best as you could to the latrines. The moment you got back into bed, you needed the toilet once again. The energy required to perform the task twenty or thirty times a day nearly did you in. We had no strength; we walked like drunk men, weaving and bumping into the walls and falling on the floor.

Then one evening, as twilight descended, I finally started feeling better and dragged myself outside to get some fresh air. The effort soon exhausted me and I had to rest against a haystack. A familiar figure approached me: 'I don't believe it! It's Ernest Löwy!' the figure said.

It was Mr Spiegel, the man whom I knew from Dunajszka Streda, who had come to the Weiss household and was always ready to help the refugees.

'I'm glad you made it,' he said. 'So many did not.' And then, in a casual manner, he said, 'You see that block? You know who has just died in there?' nodding towards one of the barracks. 'The older Weiss girl, Medy.'

He continued talking about others who had survived or perished, but he failed to realise what his comment meant to me; I almost blacked out. I thought back to the girl who had entranced me in Dunajszka Streda. Somehow I managed to hold myself together until Mr Spiegel said goodbye and went on his way. Emotionally I was destroyed. Overcome with guilt, I slipped to the floor wondering what I could have done if only I had known that she was there.

I lay on the floor for quite a while. Darkness fell. There was a very bright moon shining. I dragged myself to the door of the barracks Mr Spiegel had pointed out: the barracks where Medy was. In the moonlight I saw a number of girls, some were sitting, some lying, some half dead, but I did not enter. I could not make myself go in, I was too afraid she was no longer how she had been – as that extraordinary girl who had mesmerised me. How many times had I dreamed of her, not realising that in the end she was so close. I had not been able to help her. If only I had known of her presence, I would have helped her and she could have been alive. My despair could not have been greater.

It all seemed so vulgar but, despite being mentally destroyed, I physically started to recover so that, by the end of May, I was strong enough to be moved to the quarantine ward. This was housed in a large complex of amalgamated one- and two-storey buildings originally built for the recuperation of German soldiers during the war.

My ward seemed like an endlessly long corridor. Across from my bed was Pinki, a young Polish boy, and on my right was a middle-aged Greek prisoner with no legs who, most of the time, sat in his wheelchair playing a small octagonal accordion. He poured out mournful songs from morning till night. Sister Emma, a large but beautiful German girl, nursed me back to health, spoon-feeding me like an injured bird, though often I was too weak and despondent to eat what she brought. From my position, lying horizontal in my bed, she looked like a goddess.

For months my only thought had been to survive. Now the war was over my main fear was about my family. How many of them had suffered and perished as Medy had done? Was there somebody left to return to? Did I have a future?

'You must get your strength back,' Sister Emma said, as she tried to get a little food in my mouth. The Greek was playing a melancholy tune. 'What for?' I replied.

'So you can go and find your family.' Then, turning to the Greek, she said, 'Can't you play something more cheerful?' The Greek ignored her.

'They're all dead,' I said bluntly.

'Even if that is true, you're still alive,' she said. 'How would your mother feel if she knew that you gave up now? You owe it to her.'

The music came to a halt. 'I will never understand,' interjected the Greek with venom, 'How Germans can be killing Jews one day and then one of them can be nursing them back to life and giving them hope.'

Sister Emma turned red. 'Maybe one day,' she offered, 'you will get married and have children of your own. There will be a Jewish nation again.'

The Greek, however, pushed himself off in his wheelchair muttering, 'Crazy, crazy world.'

Every time Sister Emma passed my bed, she stopped, bent down and gave me a kiss on the forehead. Then, showing her wonderful smile, she reminded me how precious life was. She helped reinstate some faith in human nature and to nurture hope. In addition, a fellow incumbent called Susan gave me the strength I needed to face the future.

One morning I was awoken by a vision. A young girl with a cheeky smile nudged me, enquiring, 'Do you have the iron?'

I was speechless. 'No,' I apologised at length.

'Aren't you the tailor?' she asked. There was indeed a tailor in our ward.

'I'm sorry, I'm not the tailor and I don't have an iron.'

Looking puzzled she smiled at me and said, 'Well, if he comes back, can you tell him that Susan was looking to borrow the iron.'

From that day onwards Susan often came to visit me in the quarantine ward. She told me how she and her mother had survived. They had been brought to Belsen from their home town of Zneim in Czechoslovakia. Her attitude, her ever-hopeful comments and radiant face, gave me the courage to get better. And, once fully recovered, I had only one thought: I must find my family.

7

THE LAST DANCE OF A
MASS MURDERER

~

He was generally known as Schreiber, the mad kapo, a heavily built, stocky man, smaller than average height, in his mid-thirties. As the Block-Älteste (barrack superior kapo) he reigned with unspeakable cruelty over five hundred to six hundred languishing, starving, half-dead prisoners. The continuous, sickening grin on his broad, square face revealed the pleasure he drew from watching over the agony of his victims. Schreiber was the embodiment of the sadist, the classic example of how people drafted into a life of violence, hatred and fear are converted into monsters, eventually losing all sensitivity for human suffering. A probably otherwise insignificant man transformed into a mad beast.

Schreiber was Jewish. All we knew about him was that he came from Warsaw, after spending years in Auschwitz and Birkenau where, in order to impress the Nazis and survive, kapos competed with each other in brutality to fellow prisoners.

His 'headquarters' in our barrack were set up in the corner of the long windowless hut with only a small door to let some daylight in. The place was separated from the rest of us by hanging blankets nailed to the wooden ceiling. There was a small table, a stool and his bunk-bed. A heavy cricket-bat-like wooden object leaned against a large metal pot where his turnip soup was stored. He would suddenly jump from his stool, only to appear a moment later from behind the blanket, bat in hand, looking round like an actor ready to perform. For no apparent reason he would then lash out indiscriminately at us, instantly killing the helpless who would be lying at his feet with not even a sheet of paper between them and the cold ground, their eyes popping out from hunger and thirst. When life settled back to 'normal' often the bodies were just left there to rot.

Then one day he found a new method of killing. Placing himself outside the small door he was ready for us: we were herded out through the small door by another kapo, while the bat came down mercilessly. The unfortunate, the old and the weak, dropped like flies. By instinctively ducking my head, my shoulder took the full blast. The pain was excruciating but I was alive.

One day Schreiber's penknife disappeared from his table. I was standing next to him when he made the announcement. In clear Yiddish he said: 'Until now I have killed thirty to forty of you every day. Unless my knife is back on my table by tonight I promise to kill a hundred each day.'

The knife was recovered but the killing went on.

~ • ~

One day I had an idea. Taking my life in my hands, I sneaked behind the curtain, which was strictly forbidden. Schreiber looked up, ready to jump at me. As quickly as I could I made my offer: 'I want a plate of soup for some tobacco.' I had the 'treasure' wrapped in a paper in my pocket, though I can't remember when and how I acquired it. The thought of a plate of soup made me shake with excitement. Then I made a fatal mistake: instead of drinking the soup there and then, I reappeared from behind the blanket holding the mess-tin in my hand. The starving mob crowded around me their hands shoved into the tin in a desperate effort to stave off starvation. But they left me no more than a trickle to wet my parched lips.

Some days later I had another crazy idea. I collected some dry weeds, broke them up and wrapped them in the same style, hoping for another deal with the mad tyrant. Schreiber right away suspected a trick, as he opened the twisted top of the paper bag and I ran for my life. He made after me, showering a multitude of curses in Yiddish. He stumbled over some bodies, giving me enough time to make for the next barrack opposite to ours. When I entered I realised that the place was tightly piled with dead bodies to the height of a metre or more.

As I ran along on top of the corpses to reach the door at the other end, I noticed him making for the other side of the block to corner me there. I made a U-turn and reached the door through which I had entered. I was out and away, running till I dropped from total exhaustion. Looking round, I found myself in a part of the camp totally unknown to me. In the distance I noticed some handsome red-brick buildings. Dragging myself nearer and nearer, I slipped through a fence and entered one of the barracks. A babble of Hungarian speech hit my ears and I was immediately surrounded by a group of women and girls of all ages who had been deported from Budapest. There were hundreds of them, including whole families. I was going round in circles shouting the names of my own family but there was no answer. I was quickly given the food and drink from the very little these poor women had; they told me they were under the protection of the Red Cross waiting to be taken to Switzerland in some crazy exchange deal with the Nazis.

The face of a young girl, wearing glasses under an unusually high forehead, was looking down on me from a top bunk-bed. Her sad and long look caught my attention and somehow embedded itself in my memory.

I had to slip out of the women's barrack before being caught and, slipping through the same hole in the fence, I was back in my camp, ending up in a barrack half empty and with no kapo. It was the end of March or the beginning of April 1945. Camp life was becoming more chaotic in those last weeks before the liberation of the camp and the fall of the Nazi régime.

To describe the last days in Belsen would be truly impossible. It was the ultimate in human misery, suffering, degradation and humiliation. It was thought out and carried out by a murderous régime: by a society turned into a godless, mindless mob of stupid, idiotic, vicious killers. They would not stop the killing and torturing although the war was as good as lost. It was murder for the sake of murder to the last opportunity; a monstrous atrocity on a multitude of innocent, unarmed people; an unforgivable outrage against humanity; a mockery of all human feelings. This would have been the New Order in Europe ruled by the super-race or master-race; it was, in fact, the eternal and utter disgrace of a seemingly civilised nation, a disgrace which can never be obliterated.

Although Schreiber had disappeared from our barracks I would meet up with him again some time later. In quarantine every block housed different nationalities of survivors. One Sunday afternoon a group of us set out to visit the Romanian block, situated about a mile away from us. It was to become a day never to be forgotten. None of us thought we'd once more come face to face with Schreiber. It all happened so quickly.

We entered the block; the music was loud and penetrating. The floor was jammed with dancers consisting mainly of British officers and soldiers plus women of their own personnel. There were others too, forcing their way onto the crowded dance floor. We all spotted Schreiber at the same moment. He was wearing a shirt and trousers, happily waltzing with a lady towering over him. There was that unmistakable grin on his face looking up at her. He did not notice us standing at the entrance.

We were stunned, and kept looking at each other in disbelief. We agreed we had to act quickly and, instinctively, the first idea was 'Let's get him,' but no, instead we decided to do the job properly. As we came out we straight away saw two tall British MPs [military police] in their helmets and their snow-white kamaschen above their boots patrolling the area. They stopped and listened to our story. With great excitement, in a mixture of English, German and Hungarian, we tried to explain the situation. They followed us back to the block.

When we returned to the dance we found the place looked even more crowded; the noise was deafening. Schreiber, again on the floor, was doing the quick-step, practically in front of us. He did not notice or suspect anything. What made our blood boil even more was the lady he was amorously embracing was a beautiful young girl in British uniform. He, who had been so close to the Nazis and behaved in the same – if not worse – manner, was now trying to inveigle himself with the opposite side. He was certainly a man who knew about self-preservation. The following moments can not be easily forgotten. One of the officers went over to the band to stop the music. As total silence fell on the company, suddenly all eyes were on Schreiber. The transformation on his face as the officer tapped him on his shoulder could only be described as dramatic. But there was more drama to come. The girl instinctively, in a protective gesture, put her arms around Schreiber and did not let go. She was told in no uncertain way who Schreiber really was. Removing her hands, her eyes opened wide as she looked at Schreiber in horror. Pushing him towards the Englishman all she was heard to say was: 'Oh, my God!'

Outside a jeep appeared; Schreiber did not try to resist as he was shoved into the vehicle. Before driving off we were asked to appear next morning, as many of us as possible, at the British High Commissioner's office to give evidence against the kapo.

The next morning, around a hundred and fifty of us gathered outside the building. It was the end of May or beginning of June, the sun was warm but still we were shivering from the emotion and excitement. By ten o'clock the doors opened, an officer appeared, asking us who our spokesman would be. We unanimously nominated a Hungarian fellow prisoner called Pinter. Pinter was one of the few kapos, back in Wüsegiersdorf, who remained a human being throughout the war. When he reappeared half an hour or so later we were all sent home.

On the way home we contemplated the outcome of our action. We were all still residents of the quarantine when the news reached us that Schreiber was found guilty by the military tribunal; he was executed side by side with Nazi criminals.

~ • ~

How many collaborators have disappeared into oblivion? How many have lived their full natural lives without ever being brought to justice? The world will never know. The disgust and contempt we had for the collaborators far exceeded that which we had for the Germans. Looking at the brainwashed, obedient

German soldier, one couldn't help but get the impression they were dummies in uniform, whereas the collaborators, I feel, were those so desperate to save their skin that they often went above and beyond the level of cruelty meted out to us by those who knew no better. Worst of all the collaborators often turned against their own people. The question is repeatedly asked, namely, could one ever forgive these people? The clear answer is no, one could not. The generation which committed the unspeakable crimes or willingly assisted can never be forgiven. But to sustain the hatred, transferring it, redirecting it on to the succeeding generations, would be wrong. It would mean impeding any possible reconciliation among the people of the world, perpetuating hate and resentment.

Although there are neo-Nazi movements rearing their ugly heads in many parts of the world, most people today are positively different. My impression was that they did learn something from the past, that we have learnt not to be easily manipulated or brainwashed by some crazy new idea. All people seem to want is to be able to get on with their lives in a free world; in a world without slogans, political or religious, in a world free of bigotry and dogmas from the past.

In fact, I would say that, fortunately, more people in the world want peace and freedom than war and bigotry, and this was illustrated when in June 1995, on my visit to Hungary, I made a pilgrimage to the old Jewish cemetery of Papa, where my grandfather is buried. On leaving I complimented the caretaker, a simple rural man in his late sixties, on the state of the grounds and thanked him for his kind assistance. At the gate we shook hands, then he quite unexpectedly said: 'It would be a wonderful world if only people would learn to live without hatred.'

Words from a simple man worth repeating and remembering.

8

THE LONG WAY HOME

~

The British army undertook the mammoth task of organising the repatriation of the former prisoners of Bergen-Belsen. For most, the journey back home was to be no simple trip: their families had been wiped out and their possessions had been stolen, while their houses were now occupied by strangers. Many concentration camp survivors were unwelcome when they returned. It was almost as if the people they encountered thought – and some actually said – 'You should not have come back, you have no right surviving and coming back here.' What I could not have realised at the time was that it would take me almost twenty years to find a place that I could call 'my home'.

Immediately we were faced with an awesome decision: whether to start life afresh in a new country or return to the place from where we had been deported. In July 1945, Joe decided to go to Sweden but the prospect of going there did not attract me. I decided to join a Czechoslovakian transport to

Bratislava, which Susan had spoken of in the quarantine ward. After all, Bratislava was the town in which I had grown up and from there I could try to reach Budapest. In both cities I hoped to find some friends or relatives.

'Are you sure?' asked a well-intentioned British officer as I informed him of my decision. He made me feel that to return to a country that was now under Soviet occupation was clearly the wrong decision, but the desire to find out what had happened to my family overrode everything else.

When I replied that I was sure, he stared at me for a long time from behind his desk and then quietly remarked: 'I hope you know what you are doing.' The truth was I was not sure at all. I was only twenty and had not heard anything about my family since the day my father took me to the Budapest police station to serve the four-day sentence for skipping Levente service.

I gathered together some food that I had been saving over the past few weeks and, placing this in a makeshift rucksack made from a bed sheet, boarded an open goods train which was packed with other survivors who had made the same decision. There were about thirty carriages, with around forty people in each. A British army unit was to escort us as far as Prague.

At the first station we came to I clambered out of the wagon to find some water. Bending over the stand-pipe a light kick landed on my backside. I turned round; there was Susan laughing at me: 'I thought I recognised you.' I smiled back. I had hoped that she was on this transport since she came from a place called Zneim which was said to be near Prague. 'Come and join us in our wagon.'

Susan and her mother could hardly contain their joy on that journey: they were so excited at going home. I was more apprehensive at what I would find at the end of the line.

'You mustn't give up hope,' Susan said as she poked me in the ribs. 'Absolutely,' her mother agreed. These two high-spirited and delightful ladies, with their inexhaustible capacity for fun, created an atmosphere of optimism, and their natural joy was transmitted to everyone.

We needed each other's company on that grim journey through an endless panorama of gutted German villages and towns. We just gaped at the immense level of destruction: piles of rubble and twisted metal signalled where railway lines and bridges had once stood. The journey was frequently impeded by debris on the line and the train was often held up for half a day or so. If this was what Germany looked like, then what state were our own homes in? After so much suffering and destruction what hope was there for a peaceful future? Could the past ever be overcome?

Yet amongst the ruins, little children stood and waved at us as the train passed. It disturbed me to see their little faces drop as nobody returned the gesture to these children whose only crime was being born German. I couldn't help waving back.

'What are you doing that for?' demanded another survivor with bitterness.

'The little ones are innocent,' I replied. 'They cannot be blamed for the crimes committed by older people.'

Susan's mother hurried to help: 'Besides, look at all this destruction. If we expect any kind of future, then it lies in young people such as these.'

In Bayreuth, near the Czechoslovakian border, the train halted and we were told that it might be quite a while before we started moving again. As I stretched my legs on the platform, I bumped into a group of young people heading for Budapest. Talking to them, it transpired that they were non-Jews who had come from a forced-labour camp. When they invited me to the station restaurant for a drink, I could not say no. The last time I had had a beer seemed a hundred years ago. As I went to fetch Susan I saw, to my horror, the train just moving out of the station. I was stranded, my few possessions in the world gone. In desperation I approached a young American sergeant. He looked very distinguished: tall and handsome in his MP helmet. He not only spoke fluent German, but also turned out to be Jewish. He listened sympathetically – even though I still looked bloated from my force-feeding after the liberation. My story tumbled out, and I explained how I had now missed my train.

Immediately he grabbed me by the arm and together we entered the ticket-office. Sitting at a desk was the station-master, a man in his early sixties who was small and thin and looked quite dapper in his neat uniform. The American explained the situation and urged him to tell us how far the train had gone. We could hardly believe our eyes when we saw the small man jump up from his chair, point his finger at me aggressively and shout, 'I know you lot. Pinching fruit from the gardens around here. That's how you missed your train. Thieves, that's what you are, the lot of you.'

His ugly, high-pitched voice made us squirm. The American had heard enough; with one arm he pushed the German back into his chair, while drawing his gun with the other. With the gun held against the bald head of the station-master there was a tense silence, broken only by the soft moaning of the little man as the grip on his shoulder tightened. I only relaxed slightly when I saw a twinkle in the American's eye, then a hint of a smile intended for me as he loosened his grip on the station-master.

Visibly shaken, the German jumped to his feet and stood to attention. The American, towering over the small figure, approached him closer: 'Hör mal zu, du frecher Knirps' –

~

154

Listen, you insolent whipper-snapper – (du being derogatory to a stranger). He continued, 'Did you know there was a war?'

'Yes,' came the response.

'Do you know you started the war?'

'Yes' (after some hesitation), 'Yes, I do.'

'Do you also know who lost the war?'

'Yes,' came the answer.

'Then I also want you to know that from now on, you have to keep your big mouth shut and do what you are told. Now, find out quickly where our train is . . .'

The sergeant took me by the arm and rushed me through the streets of the town busy with American military personnel and vehicles. A black American truck driver, chewing gum, immediately agreed to race after the train.

At breakneck speed we drove over bumpy country roads and forty-five minutes later we caught up with the train. Speaking only very little English, I somehow managed to express my gratitude to the big man. Leaning from his cabin he gave me a big smile: 'No trouble at all, chum,' and threw me a couple of packets of Pall Mall cigarettes before speeding off. This experience of true kindness from a total stranger helped me to restore my shattered belief in humanity.

Susan and her mother stretched their arms out from the wagon and hauled me in. 'We were beginning to think we'd lost you for good,' said Susan's mother. 'Isn't our wagon good enough for you? You have to go and get your own private taxi service,' said Susan, trying to make light of the fact that she had been worried.

Despite promising to take us to Prague, the British army accompanied us only as far as Pilsen. Nevertheless, we said goodbye and thanked our saviours.

Now we noticed a change in atmosphere: the platform was

swarming with battle-weary, hungry Russians – many of them sleeping on the concrete floor with not even a paper under their heads and the ones that were awake eyed us menacingly. Fortunately, the British soldiers did not move an inch away from the train until it pulled out.

We left Pilsen in a proper train with the 'luxury' of compartments and wooden benches. Without any further adventures, the train reached Prague. Susan and her mother got out to travel on to Zneim: 'God knows what we're going to eat over the next few days,' muttered Susan's mother. 'Still, something will turn up, it always does.'

Suddenly I remembered the packets of cigarettes the American had thrown at me. 'I have an idea,' I said, proudly showing the cigarettes and dragging Susan off towards the city centre.

After the war, money was useless and the most valuable commodity was cigarettes – especially American ones. Susan and I went round shops and restaurants, swapping cigarettes for food. One cigarette bought you an entire cabbage and for two packets you got an awful lot of food. Pretty soon we had more cabbages than we knew what to do with.

Standing on the platform, Susan, laden down with fresh vegetables, bid a tearful goodbye to me as the train got under way again. 'Don't lose touch,' she cried. Unfortunately, like so many other people, that's exactly what I did do. I travelled further into Czechoslovakia feeling very alone.

We pulled into a small station where a head count was taken. On the station platform, as our names were being called out, I noticed a well-built man in the uniform of the Czech army coming towards us. He had thick wavy hair and was waving his cap over the heads of the crowd. What was more, he was waving at me and calling out my name.

'Ernest! Ernest Löwy! Don't you recognise me?' he shouted in German. 'It's me, Feldko.'

I nearly fell back in astonishment. Feldko was a distant cousin on my father's side and I had not seen him since I was a child. How he managed to recognise me in my state I shall never know, but he hugged me furiously and, as he released me from his embrace, I noticed that he was wearing a Soviet badge in his lapel and carried a revolver in his waistband.

'I've been fighting for the Red Army,' he said proudly in German. 'Are you headed for Bratislava?' I nodded. 'Good. Then we can look for our families together.'

As he steered me back into my carriage, we talked in German and Hungarian about the Russians, Belsen and my fears for the future. 'Don't worry,' he said, putting his arm around me. 'I'll look after you now.'

As we travelled further and further into Soviet-occupied territory I was glad to have Feldko at my side – not least because I did not know what to expect back home. Neither of us knew how many of our friends or family members had survived. It was beginning to dawn on me that liberation had not been the end but merely the beginning. I was even more glad of his company one starless night when our train pulled into Nove Zamki, a few hours away from Bratislava. If it hadn't been for him, I have very easily have found myself in Siberia or some labour camp or other.

~ • ~

It was past midnight and many people were asleep, huddled in corners sleeping as best as possible, or sitting upright on the wooden benches. I was using my rucksack as a kind of pillow and Feldko was next to me. Suddenly, we were woken by shouting and screaming from the other carriages and, as our eyes adjusted to the light, we saw dark figures stealthily entering our own compartment. They were coming in amid loud screams, they entered through the windows, swinging like apes, and from the corridor, snatching everyone's belongings and trying to drag people from the train. Automatically I pulled my rucksack behind my back to protect the food – one thing I had learned in the camps was to protect every morsel. As quick as a flash Feldko covered me with his body and pulled out his revolver.

He began shouting at the intruders in Russian: 'Leave us alone. We have all been fighting for the Red Army. We are on your side, comrades.' And for good measure he fired a couple of shots in the air. Luckily for us they were not returned. All went silent, except for the whimpering and weeping of the people on the train. The shadows had disappeared as quickly as they had come.

In the darkness it was impossible to know whether the danger had passed and it was only when the train started moving again that there was a sense of relief. In the grey light of the dawn we realised that, despite all of Feldko's heroic efforts, quite a few young people were missing, especially girls, and practically all our belongings were gone.

'If that's the Russians' idea of working-class solidarity, they can have it,' muttered a woman caustically. After a moment Feldko remarked: 'Still, they won the war at Stalingrad.'

Three hours later the train pulled into the Slovak capital. Nervous and exhausted, Feldko and I had no idea what to expect, our only desire was to find out what had happened to our families. At the station Jewish officials were present to welcome us and they instructed people to go and register at the Jewish Centre in the old Jewish quarter.

One of the officials stood out from the rest in his flash suit. It was my old schoolfriend, Frommer. He did not know me at first, but when I told him who I was, we embraced and I introduced Feldko as 'my guardian angel'.

'And I am a Macher' – the nickname for an influential figure in the Jewish community – Fromme said proudly, showing off his finely cut suit. 'Now I take care of you both.' And he slapped me on the back.

'Have you heard anything of my family?' I asked.

'Yes, I have wonderful news!' he told me. 'Your mother and two sisters are alive and staying in Budapest.' Then he began to look uneasy.

'And the others?' I asked, not wanting confirmation of what was written all over his face.

Frommer began to deliver the litany: my brothers Karl, Max and Fritz were still missing; but worse news was still to come: my father, Munky, Else's husband, Bernat, Hedwig, her husband, child, and my brother Karl's wife and their ten-day-old baby boy had all perished. It was only later that I was able to piece together the full story of what had befallen my family.

~ • ~

In the late summer of 1944, Munky had been taken by a group of Hungarian fascists to a small place called Fertorakos, near the town of Sporon, in north-west Hungary. There he was made to dig his own grave before they shot him in the back of the head. Munky had always been the genius of the family and the embodiment of a tzadik [a truly righteous person]. When I heard that, my thoughts went back to the years we had spent in Budapest. On Sunday afternoons, Munky and I used to take a stroll across the elegant Chain Bridge which connects Buda and

Pest, and then we walked towards the majestic Elizabeth Bridge. A visit to a 'Konditorei', smelling and tasting the fresh baking, was the highlight of the afternoon before we returned home. We used to spend the princely sum of twenty-four filler on a cream bun filled with custard. Now I would never walk along the Danube with Munky again.

I also learned the extraordinary story of Bernat, Else's husband. They had met in the village where I fell in love with Medy, but stayed together and got married. Bernat was taken to Buchenwald with my father and a neighbour called Mr Klein, who would later tell me the whole story.

During the last few chaotic weeks before liberation, many of the guards had fled, making it possible for some prisoners to escape and save themselves. Bernat had been given the chance to escape, but my father was too ill to move. Father begged Bernat to go: 'Please leave. You have a wife and child, you have a young family. My daughter is waiting for you. Save yourself.' But, as Mr Klein explained, Bernat had replied, 'How can I leave you here and go home and look Else in the face?' They died a terrible death side by side.

My sister Hedwig had lived in Györ, near Papa, where Grandfather came from. She was sent to Auschwitz with her whole family – husband and in-laws – together with the whole Jewish community of Györ. Hedwig had an infant of three who was deported with them, a gorgeous little girl. The journey in the sealed box-cars to Auschwitz took place in the heat of the continental summer – I had travelled there in the spring and, even then, the heat in the box-cars was unbearable. In summer it must have been hellish: a long, hot journey of three or four days without water. All of them arrived half dead in Auschwitz and nearly all the Jews from Györ were sent to the gas chambers on arrival. A whole community was wiped out in the last phase of the war, like so many other Jewish communities.

Yet Else, Lillie and my mother had been saved. At one point Else was taken to a brick factory outside Budapest from where she should have been deported. My sister Lillie, however, had got married in 1944 – to André Vamos – despite father's advice that she would regret this for ever. André was also what was called a Macher and personally knew the Swedish diplomat Raoul Wallenberg. When Lillie told her husband what had happened to Else he immediately went out into the night to find Wallenberg. My sister was saved at the very last minute when Wallenberg appeared and selected a number of girls to be returned to Budapest. Else was reunited with her son from her marriage to Bernat, as, fortunately, the boy had been staying at my mother's. Else managed to remain in Budapest by using the Swedish papers that Wallenberg gave her.

After Frommer had related the saga of my family I decided to go to my old home in the Schanzstrasse, a five-minute walk away from the station, instead of going straight to the Jewish Centre. To our surprise, even though the rest of the house was occupied, we discovered two of our cousins, Mädy and Trudy Donat – also having been recently liberated from a camp – living in one of the flats.

The place had been gutted, all our old belongings and most of the furniture snatched, but we warmly embraced, overjoyed at finding relatives. Mädy then said, 'Ernest I know about your family,' and I placed my finger on her lips and said, 'Mädy, I already know.'

Feldko and I left our belongings at the flat and went to the Jewish Centre to register – a big building in the Jewish quarter with ornate figures carved into the façade and a large entrance door. From behind a row of tables, volunteers wrote down our details and added our names to the lists of survivors; these lists would be circulated to other centres. Another way information was passed on was through the synagogues with the names of those 'still missing' often read out after the services. The Jewish population of Bratislava had been decimated, out of fifteen thousand people only about nine hundred had survived.

At the centre, after we had registered, we were taken into the refectory and given a big bowl of bean soup and some bread. We talked with other survivors, swapped names of those we were searching for and recounted our losses. Feldko and I ate so much that we could hardly walk back to the Schanzstrasse. When we stumbled back into the flat, Mädy and Trudy thrust another bowl of bean soup under our noses and we ate again.

I knew my future lay in Budapest with my mother and two sisters. So, the next morning, I sent a message to my mother at our old address in Budapest, hoping that she was still there, and a few days later boarded yet another train. My message, however, was not passed on, and on my arrival home two days later mother came to the door and, recognising me immediately, fell sobbing into my arms and fainted. She was still waiting for news of Karl, Max and Fritz, expecting the worst.

Karl was the first to return from a Hungarian labour camp. He was thin, lifeless and had to be nursed back to health. Max had been sent to the front at the Dnjepnr. During a Hungarian counter-attack, he had gone missing; mother had received his rucksack and feared him dead. Max's name was often read out in the synagogue from the list of missing people.

In 1946 a stranger knocked at our front door, I opened it and he asked me, 'Do you have a brother called Max?'

'Yes,' I stuttered.

'Well, he is on his way home. He was a prisoner of war.'

Mother was overjoyed when he actually turned up on the doorstep a few weeks later. Bit by bit he told us his story. Max had always been a little left-wing so, when a chance arose for him to flee to the Russian side at the front he took it. Once in Russian hands, he volunteered to go to Moscow, to a school which the Communists used to 're-educate' people. He had become one of them.

But the most miraculous escape was by my brother Fritz and his wife, Datya Pollak, whom he had met during the war. In July 1944, Datya's family were deported, but she and Fritz went into hiding in Budapest. She was in the last weeks of her pregnancy when the couple were brave enough to proceed with a most ambitious and dangerous plan.

They decided to slip out of Hungary using forged papers and make their way to Palestine. Heavily disguised, they trekked through Nazi-occupied territory. In Romania Fritz and Datya got separated but Datya, a strong-willed woman, moved on and managed to pass into Turkey. Near Adana, in open countryside, she gave birth to a girl. The next day she picked herself up, lifted her baby up and travelled on, reaching Palestine via Constantinople. Unknown to her, Fritz also managed to make it to Constantinople. He boarded a boat to Palestine, never giving up hope that he would find Datya again. The boat, however, ran into a mine and he had to jump overboard. He was rescued and eventually found Datya and his baby daughter, Ada, in Tel Aviv.

We heard the heroic story from Fritz but, while he and Datya made a clear break with the past, fought in Israel's War of Independence in 1948 and made a good life for themselves, the rest of the family back in Budapest were slower in taking their fate into their own hands.

After the War of Independence, Fritz sent us a letter asking, 'Should you try once again to integrate, to adapt to Hungarian society? The answer is no. It's the old story. It works for a while.

Then you are back in trouble again. Why impose yourself on a society which has repeatedly shown dislike and resentment towards you? Why condemn yourself to a forever-harassed minority? Is there any point carrying on praying, lamenting for redemption, pretending nothing has happened? You don't have to be persecuted any longer. Come to Israel.'

In my heart of hearts I may have known he was right. But, by now, I had become the breadwinner of the family and felt unable to break away. Else and Karl were still ill, Max taught French and English, but he could hardly support himself. The family really relied on food parcels from abroad, especially from a relative in London. We lived from day to day, but Mother was adamant about staying in Hungary.

Not only concern for my family's well-being, but also the prospect of a better future under Communism made me stay. After the camps I was finished with religion and put my faith into godless Bolshevism with its promises of fraternity and equality.

At first, conditions in Budapest were tolerable. To support the family I went into business with a friend by the name of Matushka. We had met almost immediately upon my arrival in Budapest as I was pounding the streets searching for work. We opened a little workshop in the house where we manufactured fountain-pens, but inflation got out of hand and money became worthless.

With the introduction of the nationalisation of industry we had to close down the little workshop and I got a job in the factory of a light-engineering firm. As the years went by, I worked hard, got some distinction and made good money. I bought a green motorbike – second-hand – an extravagant buy, but a necessity in a country where cars were still a luxury and public transport unreliable.

Under Communism we began to flourish and, undeniably, the régime achieved something. The slums disappeared, the crime rate sank and there was almost full employment. And, apparently, no racism.

Max often tried to get me to join the party, but for some reason I refused. My upbringing had taught me not to lose contact with the religious part of my life. This was so deeply rooted that I never lost all my belief in traditional values, despite the camps and the Communists' ban on religion in public. At home, the family still held daily prayers and our Friday night Sabbath meal, although my brother Max took the precaution of hiding our candlesticks throughout the week, just in case we had any unwelcome visitors. This helped me to maintain my belief in the traditional Jewish values and, together with my passion for singing, brought me back into the synagogue.

~ • ~

Karl was very friendly with the top cantor of Budapest – Bernard Linecky, a big handsome man from Odessa with an enormous voice. Karl and Bernard arranged for me to enter the choir of the Dohany synagogue, which was the second largest in Europe. There I met Kato Phlüger. Kato was an opera singer and had been married to the famous non-Jewish conductor of the Gewandhaus Orchestra in Leipzig, Gerhardt Phlüger. When the Nazis seized power she had left him so as not to put his career in jeopardy. Kato was a well-versed teacher. She took me on as a pupil, started my proper voice production and, after some time, I began working in synagogues, sometimes officiating on the High Festivals in smaller shuls outside Budapest.

As a result of this activity I was often called into the factory manager's office and asked to leave the religious business alone. I never did and was never promoted. Eventually I turned my back on Communism and started attending the Jewish college where rabbis and cantors were trained.

It also became apparent that anti-Semitism had not disappeared under the Communists. This, and Fritz's continued letters asking us to come to Palestine, led to renewed discussions around the dinner table. 'Maybe he is right,' I ventured once.

'And how would we get there? We have no money,' said Max, who also had other motives as he was getting more involved in his party work and had created his own circle of friends. 'Besides, Israel's no more stable than this place.'

Mother still hung on to the idea of sticking it out in Hungary. 'Perhaps things will change, get better,' she suggested quietly. 'Anyway, I'm not moving again. I'm sick of all this chopping and changing.'

It seemed as if the Löwy family, failing to realise just how bad the situation was, was again asking for 'just one more dance', but in reality the family began to disperse bit by bit.

Karl was the first to go. In 1948 he was offered a post abroad and became a cantor in Queen's Park synagogue in Glasgow. Following his example, Lillie also managed to get out of Hungary and she and her husband André went to live in Munich where they made a good life.

Actually, Karl and Lillie left just in time. By the beginning of the 1950s, with freedom of speech and individual movement becoming impossible, exit visas were like gold dust. All this created a claustrophobic feeling which added to the general frustration of the Hungarian population. They finally rose against the régime in October 1956 – a one-week spell of freedom, joy and jubilation crushed by Russian tanks.

For us, these events were sadly overshadowed by the public reappearance of anti-Semitism. Members of the old fascist organisations took to the streets shouting anti-Jewish slogans. Hungarians began to show their old colours.

After weeks of fighting, with half of Budapest in ruins, the uprising was finally put down. In the ensuing chaos and confusion thousands managed to escape over the border to the West. I was also offered that opportunity and decided to take my chance, only to find that some things still held me back.

~ • ~

In 1956 I was going out with Yetta, the daughter of a well-known rabbi. We had first met in a Budapest theatre in 1950 and even though she lived half a day's journey away from the city we would often travel to see each other. Although we had been going out together I had never asked her to marry me, perhaps she was too strong-willed and cheeky for me to cope with. 'I will never marry you because after two weeks you will call me a fool,' I once said to her.

'You are so wrong,' she replied, smiling sweetly. 'It will only take one week.'

Perhaps it was also my mother's dislike of her that stopped me marrying Yetta. On one occasion, for example, I came home late from work. 'That girl is here,' my mother said, nodding to my bedroom. I stuck my head around the door to find Yetta had fallen asleep in my bed. That night I slept on the sofa in the living-room, far away from 'that girl'.

The opportunity to escape Hungary, however, came through Yetta towards the end of the uprising. Yetta's brother and sister had joined a group of other young people who had decided to flee to freedom. We joined them, but our exodus was dogged by an injury I had sustained from a fall from my motorbike during the uprising. My ankle was so sore that I could hardly walk. The constant agony slowed us down, but Yetta refused to leave me, cursing my motorbike. We got as far as the Austrian border before being caught.

Under Russian guard we were locked in a room where we were to spend the night before being sent back to the capital.

'Tomorrow, we'll try again,' Yetta told me.

'I can't,' I said.

'What?' she replied.

'I've changed my mind. My ankle hurts too much,' I muttered, avoiding her eyes.

'We've managed so far. It's only a few more miles.'

'I can't leave my mother. Who will look after her?' I said quickly.

'That didn't seem to bother you a few days ago.'

'Well, it does now.'

'Forget your mother,' she replied tartly. 'What about me?'

'I just can't.'

'It's not your mother or your ankle that's stopping you,' she spat and stormed off to the other side of the cell to sulk.

Yetta jumped the border the next day with her brother and sister. She got as far as New York.

Yetta had been right in her suspicions about my motives. It was not just my mother that kept me in Budapest. While seeing Yetta, I had also got involved with another woman, Gizella, divorced, non-Jewish and ten years older than me. I had met her in the factory where I worked and was physically attracted to her. Our relationship could never have amounted to much but, even so, we had a four-year affair. A few hours after returning to Budapest from the Austrian border, I was with her.

On reflection I realised too late that, no matter how much I suffered with my ankle or how much I was attracted to Gizella (or even terrified of Yetta's sharp mouth), I should have fled. The chaos the uprising provided was the moment, and I had let it pass by, wanting my own 'just one more dance'.

After the uprising the situation in Hungary grew worse — even mother realised that our lot in life was not going to improve by remaining in Hungary. In 1957 my sister Else remarried and then moved to Glasgow to be with our brother Karl. Soon after, my mother managed to get a tourist visa to go and visit them. She never returned. I was left on my own, my family had moved on — Max led a separate life and I would not see him for weeks at a time.

~ • ~

Two incidents made up my mind to get out of Hungary at any price.

The first incident took place after a football match at the Nep stadium, the main football ground in Budapest, and the winning team was MTK — a team which was traditionally supported by Jews. As I walked back home, I became aware of a group of men behind me.

'Stinking Jews!' one of them started.

'Yeah, a bunch of cheats,' chipped in another.

I tried to walk faster but one of them ran up behind me and whipped off my hat. Teasing me as I tried to grab it back, he threw my hat into the gutter: 'Fetch!' Then they ran off laughing. My mind went back to the scuffles Munky and I used to get involved in with non-Jewish children at football matches in Bratislava, or just simply walking home from school. It looked as though some things would never change. I began applying for a visa and for five years I persistently tried to get the papers which would allow me to leave the country.

The second incident, in January 1961, was even more ugly. I was on holiday in the beautiful mountain landscape of the Mecsek where I met a nice young non-Jewish girl from Budapest; her name was Magda. She had blonde hair and skin like the finest porcelain. When it was time for us to go home we travelled back together. The train was full and there were not enough seats, so I stood next to her leaning against the carriage door as she sat. I was wearing my cap.

Suddenly, the door I was leaning against flew open and I only just managed to grip a handle and pull myself back inside. At first I thought that the door had not been securely closed, but then I realised that someone had opened it intentionally. The drag of air was so powerful that I had thought that was the end of me. People began to laugh, a practical joke that could have killed me – just because I was a Jew talking to a non-Jewish girl.

Moreover, word came from London that mother was quite ill. She had moved to the capital to be with Karl, who was now calling himself Charles, when he had secured a job in Hampstead.

This news and the incidents made up my mind for me and I decided to leave Hungary as soon as possible at any price. As if by a miracle I got a tourist passport valid for two months; here was my last chance.

~ • ~

My train pulled out of Budapest station on a Sunday morning in June 1961. Friends who knew of my plans to leave came to see me off. They loaded me with an unbelievable quantity of presents and there were smiles and tears as the train moved away from the platform.

Scotland was my ultimate destination, but first I went to Vienna to visit some friends. After so many years in Hungary, Vienna was another world: it was not only the standard of living which proved such a culture shock, but the freedom with which people moved, travelled and smiled at each other.

From Vienna I went to Munich to see Lillie and her family. I stayed there a number of weeks, spending whole days in the art galleries and museums. I also visited my old friends Leopold Poszoni and Zoltan Mérer from Wüsegiersdorf. They owned a chain of shoe shops in the city and were doing very well for themselves. Leopold spent many hours trying to persuade me to stay in Munich and throw my lot in with them, but I could not be dissuaded from my plans.

When it was time for me to leave, Lillie and André came to Munich central station to see me off. With one foot on the train, my brother-in-law gave me a word of advice: 'Ernest, I know you. I know your mentality. Britain is the place for you, try and settle there.' I did not know it at the time, but he was absolutely right.

In the middle of July 1961 I arrived at Glasgow Central Station, where I was met by Else, her husband, and Bernat's son who was now eighteen. He had just passed his driving test and drove us to the family home in Giffnock in his stepfather's silver Vauxhall. For a moment, when I saw Glasgow with its grey, low-flying clouds, I thought I had made a mistake. But as we drove down Fenwick Road into Giffnock suburb I fell in love with the entire area.

Unfortunately, mother had died before I could leave Hungary and not seeing her again was one of my greatest regrets. One of the first things we did after my arrival in Glasgow was to travel down to London in the silver Vauxhall to visit her grave. In London I was reunited with Charles and we discussed my future plans in his living-room. Having only a tourist visa I could not stay in Britain, but I did not want to return to Hungary. Thinking of Fritz's invitation all those years ago, I suggested going to Israel to make a fresh start in life. While we were discussing this, one of Charles's friends, Mr Goldstein, who was a very well-known choirmaster, came to the house. When he heard me singing a couple of pieces in Charles's living-room his eyes lit up and he said, 'When you come to Israel you must first come and see me.'

I left for Israel in November 1961, travelling across the Channel from Dover with a group of Jews who made Aliyah, the Return to the Holy Land. We caught a train to Marseilles where we boarded a ship for Israel. A week later I arrived in Haifa where my brother Fritz and his family were awaiting me on the dock.

~ • ~

Israel proved to be an entirely new experience. I rented a room in Tel Aviv and acquired a job in light-engineering. Life proved to be very hard. Every third week I had to do a night shift and on top of that we were suffering from a drought – water came from the taps in drips and drabs at a lukewarm temperature. It was a difficult time, but also wonderful because I could sing and further my studies in cantorial music, after having secured a cantorial position at the Bugrachov synagogue – one of the oldest in Tel Aviv. On Fridays I had to run from the factory to get washed and changed for the service.

I had not forgotten Mr Goldstein's invitation and looked him up. 'I know just the man to turn you into a great singer.' His eyes twinkled. 'Shlomo Ravitz – the greatest authority in cantorial music. Leave it with me.'

I heard no more of this musical authority until late one evening when Goldstein turned up at my front door: 'Right, now we go and see Ravitz.' I did not argue, and we walked for what must have been an hour before we came to a suburb of Tel Aviv, arriving at the man's house at about eleven o'clock.

It was a dull-looking flat on the first floor. Goldstein rapped on the door and a little man with a bald head, trying to fix his skullcap, poked his head out of the door: 'What do you want?' It didn't sound too promising. Goldstein explained to Ravitz why we were here. The old man looked at me and said rudely, 'Ach, I don't take private pupils any more. Why did you bother bringing him?'

'Just listen to him,' begged my advocate.

Reluctantly, Ravitz let us in. Looking me up and down and then planting himself in a chair he said, 'All right, then. Let's hear what you can do.'

Wanting to get out of there as quickly as possible, I sang a few notes. Ravitz stopped me almost immediately: 'I'll take him,' he said quietly.

During the next few months I learned to love that man. He was not only an excellent teacher but also a good friend. I could hardly wait for my next lesson, even though he charged me fifteen lirot each time, which was a lot of money in those days.

So things were going well for me in Israel; I had two jobs and the best teacher I could hope for. But sometimes things develop, apparently outside your control, and inevitably they shape your destiny.

Two things happened. First of all, I hurt my finger in the factory where I worked and without full mobility in that hand I could not work. I had no insurance and without insurance I had no money. So I went to my boss, Moshe, a Romanian Jew, and told him, 'Look, I have no money, I have to eat.'

Moshe said, 'Go to the doctor and if he gives you a line saying that it happened when you were working then I can help. Otherwise I can't.' Of course I could not prove that the injury occurred on the job.

Secondly, I lost my job in the synagogue. One evening one of the wardens, a man called Tenenbaum, came up to me. Hovering behind him was a younger chap who I knew was an ambitious singer. The warden, embarrassed, explained that the synagogue could no longer afford to pay what we had originally agreed. They had obviously sent him to deliver the bad news. Nodding his head sheepishly towards the other man, he commented, 'The others say he can do it cheaper.' I was furious and left the place without saying a word. Warden Tenenbaum ran out after me: 'What are you doing? You know I don't want to lose you. If you'd just take a cut . . .'

'I can't work with you people,' I sharply replied. 'I don't play games like you do.'

At that moment one of the synagogue regulars, a red-haired man by the name of Israel, appeared from around the corner. Overhearing us he said half in Hebrew, half in Yiddish, adding insult to injury, 'Let him go. He hasn't got a voice anyway.'

Things looked bleak and then I got a message from Charles saying that Pollokshields synagogue in Glasgow was looking for someone to minister their High Festival. I had been recommended and a wealthy businessman called Symie Miller had come to Tel Aviv to talk about it.

Miller was staying at the Sheraton Hotel. He made me very welcome in his suite and offered me £250 for the High Festival. That was an awful lot of money. Moreover, he gave me an open ticket, which meant that first I could travel anywhere I wanted to. Who could resist an offer like that?

The only problem was that having come to Israel on an Aliyah arrangement in which the Israeli government had paid all my travel expenses, I had to pay the money back before I was allowed to leave the country. Because I had no money I had a problem and I decided to sell everything I owned – which was not much – my shaver, my radio, whatever I had.

I travelled to Glasgow in 1962. This return meant an end to my travels.

In Scotland I found a new partner in Kathy Herman, who I had met there during my previous stay in 1961. She also came from Hungary, where she had been born in 1925. While her family was in hiding, she was arrested in 1944 and deported to Bergen-Belsen and from Belsen she was taken to Theresienstadt, which was liberated in May 1945. Kathy returned to Hungary, but left the country in 1957 to settle in Glasgow. We were married in 1965 at Pollokshields synagogue.

The strange thing was that I was sure that we had met before. And then one day I saw a beautiful school photo taken at Kathy's graduation in Budapest in 1943, immediately and unmistakably, I recognised the face of the young girl with glasses and high forehead who had looked at me from her bunk-bed in the Belsen barrack in March 1945.

Kathy recalls how, practically daily, one, two or more of the miserable-looking human wrecks would sneak into their camp and beg for food. They were really walking skeletons; she says it would be quite impossible to remember the face of a particular prisoner.

~ • ~

The job in Pollokshields was part time, so I also worked for my brother-in-law who had a very successful cash-and-carry business. I managed to save up enough money to buy a car and, finally, things were looking up.

Eventually I got a call from Giffnock and Newlands synagogue which was looking to engage a full-time cantor. At first I did not want to go full time into the ministry but, after long consideration, Kathy and I decided that it would be a good move. We were living in rented accommodation at the time and a house came with the Giffnock position. We were eager to settle down and to start a family of our own. At the same time I got a call from a very prestigious synagogue in Birmingham who approached me with a tempting offer. But in the end we decided to stay in Glasgow. Something here had clicked, I liked the city and the people, and Kathy and I were very happy. For the first time it looked as though I had a good and secure future ahead of me. I had found a 'home' and settled in Scotland for good.

9

CHALLENGING GOD

~

Kathy and I still live in Glasgow and we have two wonderful children, Judith and Robert, who both have their independent lives away from home. My wife and I are still in love with Scotland and its people. Scotland is like a sleeping beauty: there is little openly expressed prejudice here compared to other places, and the people lack cynicism and sarcasm – a trait from which other Europeans suffer an overdose. I once read somewhere that happiness can be measured by the number of friends one acquires. Making friends is not always easy, but here in Scotland it seems easier and I feel that on the basis of the number we have, our happiness is well secured.

~ • ~

People sometimes ask me whether I feel bitter and resentful about what happened before I came to Scotland. When this question is asked my mind, without fail, goes back to an army chaplain I met in Bergen-Belsen.

After the liberation of Belsen in 1945, the women of a nearby German town were daily brought to the camp in British military trucks to carry out cleaning work in and around the quarantine area. The surviving former prisoners looked on in disbelief as the German women were given cocoa and biscuits for their tea-break. Why were they being treated so well?

The feelings of resentment came to the fore when, on a beautiful sunny Saturday morning some six weeks after the liberation, a young British army chaplain donned a prayer shawl over his uniform and conducted the Sabbath service. A crowd of about sixty people, those who were strong enough to be on their feet, gathered round the chaplain and questioned him aggressively: 'What on earth do the British think they are doing? Treating the Germans so leniently with tea-breaks and biscuits?'

For a while the young clergyman listened patiently, then he calmly defused the argument: 'The thirst for revenge is the cause of endless human suffering. Do you really expect us to carry on in a manner which would only be along the same lines as the Nazis? If that is the case, then I don't know what we fought for. Allowing evil to continue would make no sense in the light of the supreme sacrifice made by the free world, by millions of individual people. Day by day the guilty ones are being brought to justice and many of them are tried and executed. But to go on punishing an unarmed civilian population would put us on a par with the Nazi killers. The time has come to bring a halt to violence, fear and hate.' At that point no more was said. The crowd disbanded quickly, returning to the blocks.

Three years later, in the spring of 1948, a public memorial service was held in the Dohany synagogue. I went along with my brother Max. A visiting rabbi ascended the pulpit to give his memorial address, and I immediately recognised him as the chaplain in Belsen.

After the service I introduced myself: 'I was one of the survivors who questioned you that morning in 1945. I have never forgotten what you said.'

With tears in his eyes, he put his hands on my face and kissed my forehead.

~ • ~

If you really want peace, you have to declare war on revenge. Endless suffering is caused by the thirst for retribution. The Nazis wanted to wipe out the Jewish nation and the other so-called 'inferior races'. But I have never looked for revenge, all I want is an end to senseless suffering.

Yet, I cannot really condemn those who took the law into their own hands after the war. Some people's losses were so profound that I cannot understand how anyone in the same position could have maintained their sanity. Cousin Feldko was one such person.

One night in 1945, after Feldko and I had returned to the house on the Schanzstrasse from the Jewish Centre in Bratislava, it was clear that Feldko was obviously in great distress. Mädy, Trudy and I were sitting round with our bowls of bean soup. We were counting our losses. Feldko, however, remained silent.

'And you, Feldko?' asked Mädy.

Then, in a broken voice, he told us how he had discovered that none of his family had survived. 'Not one single person left.'

We sat there in silence, stunned at this news. The rest of us had at least someone to go home to, to have lost everyone was inconceivable.

~

At that point Feldko jumped up from his chair and pulled out his army revolver. He started loading it slowly, one bullet at a time.

'What are you going to do?' asked Trudy nervously.

With a bitter smile on his face Feldko made for the door. We looked at each other in astonishment and fear, we knew something terrible was going to happen.

I did not see Feldko until the next night when I went to a small local synagogue. It was the eve of Tisha B'ar, the ninth of Av – a day of great religious importance to Jews. A small crowd of elderly worshippers were reciting from the Book of Lamentations of Jeremiah. I listened to them wearily as they praised God's name, seeking a meaning in the destruction of our people which we had witnessed from so close by.

'Ernest?' A hoarse whisper came from the pew behind me. As I turned round I saw Feldko, now in civilian clothes. Slowly he began to recount the events of the last twenty-four hours.

'My mother almost made it,' he said, holding his voice low. 'She went into hiding with the Novaks, friends of ours, but they say she was betrayed at the last minute by the son of a neighbour – Horace Kowalski.'

Feldko had gone to his old neighbourhood and had found grandmother Novak, who confirmed the story. His mother had indeed been betrayed by the youngest son of the Kowalski family who lived across the road. Not only that, but Kowalski had, with his betrayal, also brought the weight of the Slovak Gestapo down on the Novak family who had been punished severely for hiding Jews.

Feldko, after comforting the grandmother, went across the road to the Kowalski house and calmly tapped on the front door. It was opened by Horace's mother.

'Do you know who I am?' he asked her.

She looked at him confused, then realising who he was, said, 'No,' and tried to shut the door.

Feldko pushed it open, 'Are you sure?'

With no choice the woman replied, 'I did not recognise you in your uniform, but now I know who you are.'

'Do you know why I am here?' Feldko asked, making his way into the house and peering into every room.

'No,' she replied, expecting the worst.

'I have come to see your son, Horace.'

'He isn't here,' she replied quickly.

'Then I shall wait.'

'He may not come home at all today,' she said hastily, following him into the kitchen.

'Then who is the table set for?'

Feldko pulled up a chair by the table and laid his revolver between the crockery.

A few hours later came the sound of the key in the front door. As Horace entered the kitchen, his face apparently went white as he saw Feldko and then the revolver lying on the kitchen table. His mother by this time was in quite a state. She had been pleading with an implacable Feldko not to do her son any harm.

Embracing his trembling mother, but keeping his eyes on Feldko, Horace said, 'Don't worry, Mother. Leave us. I'll sort him out.'

As she left, Feldko said to Horace, 'Thanks to you I have no mother to embrace.' As the mother closed the kitchen door the last thing she heard was a shot. When she came back Horace was lying on the floor and Feldko was halfway out of the front door.

Feldko told me all this as the handful of men in the synagogue were speaking from Jeremiah. It was the prophet

Jeremiah who was supposed to have been an eye-witness to the agony and despair of his own people, but had still retained his faith in God and the Covenant. For me, having just returned from the camps where I had witnessed the ultimate degradation of the Jewish people and listening to Feldko's story, their prayers made little sense.

'Within a few hours,' Feldko informed me, 'I will be leaving this country for good. I am going to Palestine.' And with that he left. No one ever heard from Feldko again.

~ • ~

There is no doubt that what Feldko did was wrong but, listening to the old men's prayers, I could neither condemn nor condone the man who had taken the law into his own hands. The world of those worshippers in that tiny synagogue reeked with cosiness, facile reasoning and easy answers. More than six million people had been wiped out, but they asked God's forgiveness for their transgressions which had brought about the Holocaust.

My father would always say, 'Mein Kind, don't worry. God will look after us. God will provide.' If he had lived he might have believed that the Holocaust was God's punishment of the erring Jewish people. Orthodox Judaism is built on the promise of divine reward and punishment: God will return to lead his people to the Holy Land once they have learned to tread the path of righteousness. Originally the Jews had been expelled from the Holy Land for blaspheming God. They can only redeem themselves if God punishes them for their transgressions.

During the war the punishment was so great that many asked at the time how much longer they would have to suffer before God brought it to an end. The Yiddish rabbi in Budapest who threw up his arms to God at the end of 1943 in front of Father and myself was one of them. In desperation he had challenged God, demanding an end to the suffering. His cries remained unanswered.

In Wüsegiersdorf, sitting half-dead on a latrine and watching the suffering all around me, I had done the same. I threw up my arms and said, 'If there is a time to act, God, then it is surely now'. But my pleas remained unanswered too. When Helmut told me on the train to Belsen that he was finished with religion, I truly meant it when I replied, 'So am I'.

Today I know I am finished with the old, blinkered religious dogma. There is no such thing as divine reward or punishment, there are only the consequences of our actions — no sin is so great to have merited the Holocaust, no sin warranted the death of all those innocent children. It was a man-made, not God-made, phenomenon. We cannot wait for the Messiah to bring an end to suffering because there is no Messiah to come. But there still can be a messianic age and only ordinary people can bring that about.

In our world we may be on the brink of a messianic age. Over the past few years mankind has made great steps towards international peace. Yet a lot more needs to be done. In modern society we continue to witness xenophobia — that unfounded fear and resentment of the stranger and the minorities that live among us. That fear arises from the fact that the stranger challenges our supremacy. His hard work brings success of which we are envious, resentful of the fact that his existence challenges our status.

Minorities are not completely blameless. Sometimes they do not easily integrate into society; my own family in Bratislava was guilty of that. Self-segregation enforces unfounded fears and hostility within the greater community. Each person must be part of society, without giving up his identity, values or traditions. And each person must recognise the validity of each other's beliefs and religions. There is a fundamental human right to be as different from each other as we please, each human being is unique. Instead of seeking conformity we must turn the whole thing upside down and recognise that differences can be wonderful in adding colour and spice to our lives.

Diversity should be the norm. If you want a rich and full society then everybody should have the right to their own little peculiarities. The more colour there is, the more beautiful the world becomes. Different people learn from each other and their lives are enriched. In Glasgow I have learned many things from the Scots and I hope they have learned something from me. Only together can we build a brighter and safer world. Bratislava was a diverse community but the differences were feared, not celebrated. Instead of life being enriched, it was degraded and people became bestial.

I do not question the very basis of the Jewish faith. They are true and enduring. But, for me, Judaism is more a way of life than a religion and the most important single element in Judaism, as written in the Torah, is 'Love your neighbour as yourself'. God is implanted within the human being. One can only serve Him through His people.

When people ask me where God was in Belsen, I say, 'He was there down in the dust with me. As the psalmists say: "*Imo anochi vzara*" – I am one with you in trouble.' People ask me, 'What then is God?' My reply is, 'God is part of us. He is the imperceptible in our existence, the spiritual dimension in us, expressing Himself through our minds.' As the writer Mordechai Kaplan puts it: 'When we pray we speak to the highest within ourselves.'

I do say my family prayers, counting the blessings for the life I have now, and I have a lot to be thankful for in spite of the past.

In the final outcome I feel my father would not disagree with my statement that religion means making God an ever-present reality.

The Nazis acted unchecked by any moral or religious constraints and proved to what depths humanity might sink once in the hands of the godless.

Central to Judaism are the Ten Commandments. They have become the basis of civilisation; they also form the core of a disciplined existence.

In the Jewish community my thoughts sometimes cause consternation. Many prefer not to think for themselves, but just blindly follow ancient dogma. I once had a young rabbi in my house who listened silently as I told him about my conception of religion, of God. He did not say a word; perhaps he knew I was right, but preferred not to be deterred from his own beliefs.

Referring to my father's unconditional adherence to his faith, 'Let it be so, mein Kind', mother advised. 'We don't want to rock the boat. Anyway, your father sinks his head into the mystics of the holy books instead of facing life's realities. I wish he would learn it is time to take his destiny into his own hands.'

My hope was that, after the Holocaust, a new humanity would arise. These hopes were not totally unfounded. We do live in a better world. We must not allow religion to be misused again, letting it increase suffering, promote intolerance or justify war. Neither do I accept that we preach a passive acceptance of misfortune and evil.

Regarding the future, it would be well for all of us to heed my father's favourite motto, Proverbs 22:6: 'Train up a child in the way he should go; when he grows older he will not depart from it.'

EPILOGUE

CHRONOLOGY OF ERNEST LEVY'S LIFE AFTER THE WAR

~

1945

Belsen is liberated. Ernest discovers that Medy was also at the same camp, but had died just a few hours before he received this news.

A British chaplain makes a great impression upon Ernest with his attitude towards human misery and revenge.

Having recovered from hunger and illness, Ernest has to decide on the future. He eventually decides to return to Czechoslovakia in a bid to find his family. In Bratislava he learns that 900 Jews out of a pre-war population of 15,000 have survived. He also hears from an old friend that his mother and two sisters are still alive in Budapest.

He immediately heads for Budapest where he discovers that his brother, Karl, is also alive, but his brother, Max, was taken prisoner by the Russians and is believed to be dead.

Ernest learns that his brother, Fritz, and his pregnant wife,

Datya, had travelled illegally to Palestine. In Romania the couple had become separated and Datya had travelled on to Turkey where she had given birth and then continued on to Palestine. Fritz meanwhile, had boarded a ship to Palestine that had hit a mine. Miraculously he was fished out of the water and was reunited with his wife in Tel Aviv.

Ernest's sister, Else, had been on the verge of deportation but was saved by the Swedish diplomat Raoul Wallenberg. Her husband, Bernat, had perished in Buchenwald alongside Ernest's father, Leopold Löwy. Bernat had been given the chance to escape but refused to leave Leopold to die alone. Ernest's sister, Hedwig, along with her husband, his family and their own small child had all died in Auschwitz. Ernest's brother, Alexander (Munky), was forced by Hungarian fascists to dig his own grave before he was shot.

In Budapest Ernest tries to settle back to 'normal life' and gets a job in light engineering.

~ • ~

1946

News arrives that Max is alive in Russia as a PoW.

~ • ~

1947

Fritz writes to Ernest and tells him that he should not try to assimilate in Budapest again but come to Palestine and start a new life among his own kind. Ernest, instead, puts his faith in the new Communist régime, with its message of egalitarianism. His war-time experiences have caused him to lose his religious belief.

~

Despite the official party line, anti-Semitism continues. Ernest gradually loses faith in the Communist idealogy and returns to the Jewish faith.

~ • ~

1948
Ernest's brother, Karl, emigrates to Glasgow to be followed later by Else and her family.

~ • ~

1956
The Hungarian uprising. Ernest tries to escape across the border with a Jewish girlfriend but is caught and thrown in prison by the Russians. On release, his girlfriend succeeds in getting across the border, but Ernest has second thoughts and returns to Budapest because of another woman he is involved with there.

Ernest remains in Hungary despite the increasing anti-Semitism and eventually he becomes a refusenik [one who is not granted an emigration visa by Soviet authorities].

~ • ~

1961
Ernest, realising that the situation in Hungary is becoming even more hopeless for Jews, unexpectedly receives a tourist passport, valid for two months. He immediately heads for Glasgow, lives with no intention of returning to Hungary.

~ • ~

1961

After a brief stay in Glasgow, Ernest decides to emigrate to Israel where he stays with his brother, Fritz. Ernest receives professional vocal training and becomes a cantor.

~ • ~

1962

Not content with the idea of settling in Israel, Ernest returns to Glasgow and is offered a position as cantor in Pollokshields synagogue, which he accepts.

~ • ~

1965

Ernest marries Kathy Herman. Originally from Hungary she had also been in Bergen-Belsen and then Theresienstadt. She had left Hungary after the uprising of 1957. They now live in Giffnock, Glasgow, where Ernest continues his vocation as cantor and seeks to redefine, practise and preach a spiritual and moral way of life in today's world.